DIGITaL
nomads

HOW TO LIVE, WORK AND PLAY AROUND THE WORLD

ESTHER JACOBS & ANDRÉ GUSSEKLOO

www.digitalnomadbook.com

© 2016 Esther Jacobs & André Gussekloo

Cover design
By 'Levro'; Sergey Myshkovskiy (Kyiv, Ukraine), s.myshkovski@gmail.com, via 99designs.com
Photo Esther: by www.eefphotography.com
Photo André: Henco Jonker

Interior design
Marieke Rinzema & Nina Roepers, Fuig text and design,
The Netherlands; mariekerinzema@gmail.com

Authors
Esther Jacobs: www.estherjacobs.info
André Gussekloo: www.andregussekloo.com

Editor
Almondie Shampine, www.almondieshampine.com

Publisher
Self-published; printing on demand via Amazon's www.createspace.com

Print book ISBN 978-90-6523-128-4
Ebook (ePub/Kindle): ISBN 978-90-6523-138-3
PDF ISBN 978-90-6523-138-3

Disclaimer

The authors are not responsible for misfortunes resulting from reading this book: jet lags, culture shock, broken relationships, lost jobs, spent pensions, etc. We do like to take credit for new friends, broadened worldviews, increased happiness, and the like. Also, we will gladly accept shares in successful digital nomad startups resulting from this book…

Sources

The information in this book is mainly based on our own experiences and tips from other digital nomads. Contributions and quotes are properly credited. Some of the more in-depth research was done via internet. Where possible we mention the source. Getting to the original source was sometimes difficult, because the same information appears on various sites and blogs. So if you feel we might have used original information from your website or blog and failed to correctly mention its source, please let us know (as detailed as possible), and we'll update and give proper credit.

The secret of happiness

is freedom.

And the secret of freedom

is courage.

Thucydides

TABLE OF CONTENTS

WORK 172

PLAY

DIGITAL NOMAD STORIES

Motivational speaker **Esther Jacobs** (1970) got 34
'fired' from her country for traveling too much.
The Netherlands de-registered her, because her
way of life 'did not fit the system', even though
she owned a house, paid taxes, and ran her own
business. Esther managed to turn this into an
opportunity, and is now an advocate for the digital nomad lifestyle. The Dutch government now
even seeks her advice on the topic!

Rob Greenfield (1986) is an American adven- 54
turer, environmental activist, and an entrepreneur on a mission to entertain, educate, inspire,
and give back to the world. He traveled through
the USA without a penny. He explains why it's OK
not to pay taxes.

Co-author **André Gussekloo** (1980) and his girl- 57
friend Marta took their laptops and their cat on
a trip to Thailand. The experiment proved successful, so they also traveled through Central
America. They now live on Lanzarote with their
baby boy, but still like to escape for a few months
a year.

Freelance translator **Martina Russo** (1989) from 70
Italy worked from the Galapagos Islands, and
other unusual places. She loves to immerse herself in nature and likes to do extreme sports
wherever she travels.

DIGITAL NOMAD STORIES

Daniela Ramos (1994) is a blogger and copywriter from Mexico. She has lived in the US and the UK and writes mainly in English. By camping, staying with friends, and hitchhiking, she manages to cut costs and visit many countries per year.

96

Jacob Laukaitis (1994) is an online entrepreneur, avid traveler, SEO specialist, and an occasional tech writer. Originally from Lithuania, he learns something new in every country he visits, and he is always looking for business opportunities.

120

The Kortman family traded their house for life on the road. Since March 2014, the family of six has been traveling around the world, moving every three months or so. Dad sustains their family (and three full-time employees) with a digital marketing business.

148

Tal Gur (1975) created financial freedom in one year after being in $34,000 of debt. He now helps others to achieve the same freedom. Originally from Israel, he's lived, worked, and traveled in over 50 countries across six continents. His main focus is personal development.

157

Vera Ruttkowski (1980) is a virtual assistant from Germany. She lived on Tenerife for two years, and is now exploring Asia for a taste of the digital nomad life.

169

DIGITAL NOMAD STORIES

Laura Viviana (1983) traveled a lot in her early twenties, and then found a dream job as a copywriter on Wall Street. So how did she end up across the table from Esther in Southeast Asia? In this interview, Laura openly shares her journey, ups and downs and learnings. And indeed, she has a way with words...

Hilda and Bas from the Netherlands sailed with their small kids to –and through– the Caribbean. At first the project seemed too big and bold and was doomed to remain a dream. But when they made a hypothetical plan, it suddenly seemed realistic and they decided to just do it.

Half Spanish, half Dutch **Sylvia Lorente van Bergen Henegouwen** (1976) is as European as they get. She studied in France, lives in Germany, and has helped develop over 400 mobile apps. She took a sabbatical from her job as a startup mentor to travel to 12 world cities in 12 months.

Marcus Meurer (1977) and Feli Hargarten (1981) run a German travel blog and organize digital nomad conferences and digital nomad workations around the world.

INTRODUCTION BY CHRIS GUILLEBEAU

Something strange happened a dozen years ago: the world split open. In a short period of time, a large group of people began making a living (and crafting a life) very differently than anyone had ever done before. They forged new lives without a fixed address. They set out to become intentionally homeless. Without much in the way of planning, they ventured to new lands and set up shop, only to leave again and move somewhere else.

Sure, there have always been traders and nomads—just look at the merchants of Libya or China from centuries ago. But those merchants didn't have MacBooks. They traveled and traded only with people they met along the way. If they wanted to journey long distances, it required a great deal of time and money.

These days, being a digital nomad presents countless opportunities that the merchants of old didn't have. From the pulse of your phone or laptop, you can connect with people all over the world. You can earn an income in one country and spend it in another. And as a bonus, you no longer have to travel by camel.

There's just one small challenge. Becoming "location independent" is highly possible (and many, many people have done it), but it's not always easy. You'll want to follow the age-old advice from Seneca: before beginning, prepare carefully.

That's how this book will help you. It's designed to be accessible and practical. You can read it in a day, but it can be your guide for a complete lifestyle change.

What does this mean for you? It means it's your turn to join the club. If you've been looking in from the outside, eager to choose your own adventure, you now have two important tasks to complete. The first task is to turn the page. The second task is to begin packing your bags.

Chris Guillebeau
Portland, Oregon
USA

Chris Guillebeau is the New York Times bestselling author of *The Happiness of Pursuit*, *The $100 Startup*, and other books. During a lifetime of self-employment, he visited every country in the world (193 in total) before his 35th birthday. Every summer in Portland, Oregon he hosts the World Domination Summit, a gathering of creative, remarkable people. Connect with Chris on Twitter, on his blog, or at your choice of worldwide airline lounge.

> Chrisguillebeau.com

Once in a while it really hits people that they don't have to experience the world in the way they have been told to.
– Alan Keightley –

WELCOME TO THE FUTURE!

Not too long ago, companies needed their employees in one location to enable full-scale industrial production. But today, they've begun to understand that as long as employees deliver results, their physical location and work hours don't matter.

As a result, a new class of employees has emerged; people whose work is completely location and time-independent. They spend their time traveling while working — taking freelance assignments from the tropical island of Aruba, running their own businesses from Berlin or working for an employer in California from Buenos Aires.

My grandparents, who were born and raised in the Soviet Union, had a very simple idea of success. They wanted to find one job, and do it for the rest of their lives. For them, this was ideal because it allowed them to stay firmly inside their comfort zones. They wanted life to be uncomplicated and predictable: Go to the office at 9 am, make sure you look like you're busy all day, stay under the radar, and leave at 5 pm. Two generations and a few decades later, much has changed. I hate simple and predictable; I dislike offices; I don't want to stay under the radar; and I love being outside my comfort zone.
— Jacob Laukaitis —

People are much happier when they spend their time doing things they're passionate about while living where they want. As a digital nomad, you can do just that. If you like to play golf, you can travel from one famous golf course to another. If you're into sailing, you can charter a yacht in Turkey and sail to Croatia with your friends.

Dutch nomad Pieter Levels figured out how important factors like travel time, expenses, cost of living, Wi-Fi, safety, climate and entertainment are when deciding on your next destination. He created NomadList.com, which is an overview of the best cities to live and work remotely, as well as the chat community #nomads (hashtagnomads.com) and Nomad-Forum.io. Pieter is pioneering the new lifestyle. He only communicates through Twitter (professing that email is dead), and he has very specific ideas on how remote work and digital nomads will evolve in the next 20 years.

Pieter Level's predictions for 2035:

* 60% of the working population will be freelancing; there will be far less people in corporate jobs.
* 1 out of 3 freelancers will be digital nomads. It will be more common to find jobs that you can do from wherever you want. As a result, people will not only be able to work from home or while traveling, but also from small villages if they prefer that lifestyle.
* Depending on your definition, there will be about 1 billion digital nomads. A real remote generation.
* Internet speed will increase up to 6G. This will make speed basically irrelevant.
* Big cities are going to claim more power. (They might even introduce city tax...) Cities are going to compete to attract digital nomads, for example by offering green cities, fast internet, and other perks.
* The price of flights will drop dramatically and new planes will be much faster. It will be super cheap and will only take a couple of hours to fly anywhere.

- ⭐ Due to these lifestyle changes, marriage rates will continue to drop, and there will be fewer house ownerships and mortgages.
- ⭐ More connected people worldwide and more traveling would also mean more international friendships, more online dating, and mixed race relationships.
- ⭐ Children won't need to go to school (because they can learn online), resulting in an increase in homeschooling.
- ⭐ Universities will offer more online courses, combined with on-site working sessions.

Basically, we are still at the start of a work revolution, but the digital nomad era is already taking shape. The pioneers of this lifestyle are no longer seen as 'outcasts', but are admired and copied. More and more people consider these pioneers role models, paving the road for the next generation.

With the publication of Timothy Ferriss's The 4-Hour Workweek, in 2009, it became cool to "Escape 9-5, Live Anywhere, and Join the New Rich." His bestseller is sometimes nicknamed 'the digital nomad bible'.

Chris Guillebeau visited all 193 countries in the world before his 35th birthday. He turned this lifestyle into a business by writing a number of bestsellers, such as The $100 Startup. He created The Art of Non-Conformity, a travel blog, initiated the Travel Hacking Cartel, and organizes the annual World Domination Summit; a worldwide gathering of remarkable people.

Natalie Sisson left New Zealand in 2006, travelled the world, and lived out of her suitcase. She wrote her bestseller, The Suitcase Entrepreneur, and now runs an online business that allows her to be location independent while generating a six-figure income. She is an inspiring example to her army of 'freedom fighters'.

The digital nomad lifestyle has even become a status symbol. Tim, Chris and Natalie have many followers who are trying to design their own dream life. Some nomads gather their own following by sharing their experiences, choices, and inspirations.

So, if you've ever dreamed of exploring the world, this is the time to do it. It won't require sacrificing your career, on the contrary; it might even boost it!

WHAT IS A DIGITAL NOMAD?

The first digital nomad was probably writer Steve Roberts, who started his journey through the United States in 1983. During his eight-year road trip, Roberts equipped his recumbent bicycle with more and more gadgets: a radio connection, a mobile telephone, a battery, a computer, and a keyboard that consisted of four keys on each side of his handlebar.

At the time, digital nomads weren't called as such. Instead, the term technomad was used by Roberts and those he inspired. Even today, there are still self-proclaimed technomads, most of whom are US citizens and drive around the Americas in RVs or campervans.

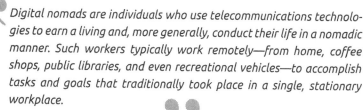

Digital nomads are individuals who use telecommunications technologies to earn a living and, more generally, conduct their life in a nomadic manner. Such workers typically work remotely—from home, coffee shops, public libraries, and even recreational vehicles—to accomplish tasks and goals that traditionally took place in a single, stationary workplace.
– Wikipedia (bit.ly/wiki-dn) –

Defining the term 'digital nomad' is a challenge. Take a look at the situations below. Would you consider someone a digital nomad who:

★ works online and travels twelve months per year?
★ works online and travels three months per year?
★ travels twelve months per year but makes only a small part of their money online?
★ is based in one spot, but makes a lot of trips, always taking their work with them?
★ changes countries every six months, living in long-term rentals?

As you can see, it's hard to draw the line between a settled and a nomadic life. And it's equally hard to decide when someone is 'digital enough' to be deemed a digital nomad. That's why we won't spend too much energy on defining what a digital nomad is. Instead, we propose that anyone may call himself or herself a digital nomad. That's right – you too. Now let's get to work, shall we?

ABOUT THIS BOOK

This book is an example of what digital nomads can do. We, André and Esther, had never met when we decided to write this book. It was completed in different parts of the world, in different time zones, and with only two 'real life' meetings.

In 2014, Esther published her 'Handbook for World Citizens' about her struggles with the Dutch bureaucracy, 'forcing' her to adopt the digital nomad lifestyle (more on page 34). She got so many questions and reactions, also from aspiring nomads outside of the Netherlands, that she decided to address an international audience. Merely translating the book was no option, however, because much of Esther's experiences were based on Dutch laws. Also, the developments in the digital nomad world were accelerating at such a pace that translating the 2014 book would only result in outdated information. So, she endeavored on a completely new book, Digital Nomads, and announced her new project on Facebook.

André already ran the successful Dutch website www.werkenvanuithetbuitenland.nl (the URL translates as 'working from abroad') and was considering an international version of the platform. When we exchanged ideas on Facebook, the idea of writing the book together popped up. In a few emails, we found our shared passion for the digital nomad lifestyle and decided to go ahead. Without any formal meetings, financial or legal agreements, any paperwork or other hassle, the project was created. The first thing we wrote was the back cover text. This forced us to decide how we would structure and present the book. Then we had the cover designed through a contest on 99designs.com; a first for both of us. More than 50 designs were submitted, and together we coached the winning one to its current form. We collected useful websites, quotes and articles in Evernote and Dropbox. Then we used Scrivener to outline and write parts of the book. We edited in Google Docs until everything came together.

We got to know each other a bit through occasional Skype sessions. André was mainly in the Canary Islands, because his son Diego was born there, about halfway through the book. Esther 'commuted' between a rural farm in Mallorca and different friends' houses in Amsterdam at first and then cruised to South America on the first nomadcruise (more info on page 273).

We first met 'for real' in Barcelona (a bit weird, because we'd already been working together for a few months). During the first DNX Global Conference in Berlin, we had some time to really work together, interview other nomads, and finally sync our Scrivener and Dropbox files (which got hopelessly messed up again afterwards, because Esther was rarely in a place with fast internet). So, we can assure you that during the writing of this book, we experienced all digital nomad 'problems' (see page 161) first hand.

We divided this book in three parts: trying to fit all information and tips about the digital nomad lifestyle in: LIVE, WORK, and PLAY.

LIVE

How to make it possible. Commitment. Habits required to become a digital nomad. How do you prepare for life on the road? Strategically design your international life. Minimize to the max.

WORK

How to finance your life. Purpose. What's it like to work remotely? What kind of jobs can you do? How can you increase your productivity to gain more freedom?

PLAY

How to enjoy. What to do with your new-found freedom. Where to go. How to meet other digital nomads. Mini retirements, workations and repositioning cruises. Giving back, sharing. What is it that you really live and work for? How to link LIVE, WORK and PLAY and put it all together.

Throughout the book various digital nomads share their experiences, eye-openers, tips and successes.

Most topics are specific to (aspiring) digital nomads, but many tips are also interesting for more sedentary readers or 'couch nomads'. For example, by minimizing your expenses, possessions, and work, you can create more time, energy, and freedom, which you can then spend any way and any place you like, even at home.

You can read everything in the order presented, but you can also pick and choose the parts that are relevant to you right now, and come back to the rest later.

We wish you a lot of fun reading, preparing, travelling, and sharing with others.

André Gussekloo

Esther Jacobs

Canary Islands

Brazil

January 2016

PS: The world is our playground; let's take good care of her!

LIVE

To travel is to live

Hans Christian Andersen

EIGHT REASONS TO BECOME A DIGITAL NOMAD

Why would you become a digital nomad? We have all been asked this question when we declared our location-independence. Your parents, your boss, or your best friend; they all wonder why you would want to trade your comfortable life back home for a succession of unknowns.

The less they have traveled themselves, the more likely they are to resist and question your new lifestyle. Some will project their fears onto your situation. This can be frustrating, but there is no way you can change their mind, just like they can't change yours. You've got your reasons for your decision and they've got their reasons to be insecure. Whether it's for your or their sake, we've compiled a list of eight common motives:

1) BREAK FROM THE TEMPLATE LIFESTYLE

The universal recipe for success seems well defined: study hard, get a respectable job, buy a house, get married, have a family, save up for your kids' studies, retire, and maybe, just maybe, make that round-the-world trip. It has, sort of, worked for the generations before, so why change or even doubt this template?

Times have changed. Jobs-for-life are a thing of the past. Houses aren't the sure-fire investment they used to be. Divorce rates surge. Pensions and life-long jobs aren't safe or guaranteed anymore. A career is no longer the ultimate goal in life. Lack of freedom is making us unhappy and restless. No wonder why more and more people wake up and question the status quo. We are the first to admit that digital nomad life may not provide all the answers, but it sure makes a lot more sense to follow your own bliss than someone else's.

Normal is getting dressed in clothes that you buy for work and driving through traffic in a car that you are still paying for - in order to get to the job you need to pay for the clothes and the car, and the house you leave vacant all day so you can afford to live in it.
– Ellen Degeneres –

2) LIVE CHEAPER

How does living in a villa with a swimming pool sound? How much healthier would you eat if you didn't have to cook your own meals or live on fast-food? How much time could you free up if someone else washed and ironed your laundry and did your cleaning? Would you be more fit if you could afford a personal trainer? Chances are, there is a cheaper place on the planet than the country you are currently in.

Making money in a relatively strong currency –say, dollars or euros– enables you to live like a king or queen in countries with a weaker currency. When you move to a place with lower costs of living, you can change your lifestyle to suit your goals. Timothy Ferriss, author of the famous '4-Hour Workweek', called this *geo-arbitrage*.

Since the cost of living is lower, you can choose to work less. Or you can work as much as you did back home and save up for your travels. Another possibility is to indeed live a lot more luxuriously than you were used to. Many nomads who chose to work from Thailand report eating out all the time and taking daily foot massages; this is only one of the many destinations where your dollar or euro stretches further than back home.

3) FOLLOW THE WEATHER

Whether you are from Tel Aviv or Trondheim, chances are you'd love to escape the local climate from time to time. You don't have to be a snowboarder to appreciate the snow or a surfer to stick to tropical beaches. When your work makes you location-independent, you get to escape the smog, traffic, heat or cold, and travel to wherever you feel best. And when the weather (or your mood) changes, you just pack up and go again.

One thing is sure about my future travel plans: avoiding the winter, following the sun, and spending as much time as possible at the beach, is what makes me happy.
– Vera Ruttkowski –

4) WORK FROM INSPIRING LOCATIONS

You can work from anywhere, as long as you can find an internet connection. You are not bound to your rental apartment (or villa, for that matter), but you can choose any location that best matches your state of mind or activities. For informal brainstorming sessions, go to a busy coffee shop. For fast Wi-Fi, hire a desk at a coworking office. For maximum concentration, visit the local library. You could even work poolside if you wanted to – although it won't take long before you find out that pools and beaches make for photogenic, rather than productive, workplaces.

5) TRAVEL THE WORLD

Maybe you are one of many who feel most alive when they're on vacation. Fortunately, you were born in the internet age where, instead of alternating months of work with a week-long vacation, you can be exploring new destinations permanently.

Let's be realistic, though; you will be working a lot of the time. But instead of spending your afternoons watching TV and your weekends in the local pub, you can spend your free time diving, surfing, hiking, meeting new people, or simply lazing by the beach.

So why postpone your round-the-world trip until you're too old to enjoy it? You better start making your bucket list of countries to visit, because you'll soon be able to travel there.

6) MEET LIKE-MINDED PEOPLE

You may have heard the saying that in many ways you are the average of the five people you spend the most time with. If you usually surround yourself with people who are stuck in the location-dependent 9-to-5 rut, chances are that you are severely limited in your thinking and your possibilities. By moving to places where digital nomads are working, living, and playing, you will notice how your conversations change, opening your mind up to the boundless possibilities of online entrepreneurship and cultural diversity.

7) GROW!

Self-development is one of the beneficial side effects of traveling. When you leave your trusted environment, you open yourself up to new experiences. Some will be great; others will be challenging. These challenges are what make you grow as a person. Learning new languages, meeting people from different cultures, and visiting or living in remote places, will give you new tools. Having to manage yourself workwise, deal with distractions, find focus amidst chaos, decide where to go, when and with whom to go, will shape your character. Warning: you will never be the same and you can never go back to who you were before.

8) BECAUSE YOU CAN

We live in exciting times. None of the generations before had the opportunity to travel as fast and as cheap as you can. None of your parents, grandparents or great-grandparents could do their work on laptops, let alone surf the web. Every day, new apps, gadgets, and other technology and jobs are invented that make life and work even more easy and more fun. So why wouldn't you take advantage of this incredible freedom? We're not saying you owe it to previous generations, but they would probably do the same if they were in your shoes.

The measure of intelligence is the ability to change.

Albert Einstein

TEST: ARE YOU A DIGITAL NOMAD?

The digital nomad lifestyle may sound cool and exclusive, but in fact anyone could live like this – that's one of the reasons we wrote this book. At its most basic level, all you need in order to be location-independent is a laptop and a way to make money on the internet. But that's not all. Your attitude may be your most important asset. Take the test. Do you have what it takes to be a digital nomad?

Applies to me	yes	maybe	no
It's easy for me to make new friends.			
I love coming home after my vacation.			
I don't like surprises.			
I have or want children.			
Wherever I am, I ask for the Wi-Fi password.			
It's not where you are; it's who you're with.			
I prefer a clear distinction between my work and my private life.			
25 days of vacation a year is more than enough.			
I can focus very well, and am not easily distracted.			
A steady job is what gives me the most security.			
Cities or beaches? It's hard for me to choose.			
I'm good at managing deadlines and appointments.			
I'm very attached to my material possessions.			
My suitcase is always too heavy when I travel.			
I always see business opportunities.			
I'm a control freak. I like things to be safe and predictable.			
Home is where the laptop is.			
I'm always looking for new inspiration and experiences.			
I don't see problems, but rather I see challenges.			
The idea of leaving everything behind freaks me out.			
I'm ready for adventure!			

Calculate your score on the next page.

SCORE YOUR TEST

Applies to me	yes	maybe	no
It's easy for me to make new friends.	2	1	0
I love coming home after my vacation.	0	1	2
I don't like surprises.	0	1	2
* I have or want children.	0	0	0
Wherever I am, I ask for the Wi-Fi password.	2	1	0
It's not where you are; it's who you're with.	2	1	0
I prefer a clear distinction between my work and my private life.	0	1	2
25 days of vacation a year is more than enough.	0	1	2
I can focus very well, and am not easily distracted.	2	1	0
A steady job is what gives me the most security.	0	1	2
Cities or beaches? It's hard for me to choose.	2	1	0
I'm good at managing deadlines and appointments.	2	1	0
I'm very attached to my material possessions.	0	1	2
My suitcase is always too heavy when I travel.	0	1	2
I always see business opportunities.	2	1	0
I'm a control freak. I like things to be safe and predictable.	0	1	2
Home is where the laptop is.	2	1	0
I'm always looking for new inspiration and experiences.	2	1	0
I don't see problems, but rather I see challenges.	2	1	0
The idea of leaving everything behind freaks me out.	0	1	2
I'm ready for adventure!	2	1	0

* This question does not earn any points. Many nomads travel with kids. Having a family does NOT prevent you from travelling (see page 145).

TEST RESULTS

So, where do you stand? How do you score on the nomad scale?

0-10 points: Couch potato

How did this book ever find its way to your hands? Having scored 10 points or less, it looks like the only nomading you'll ever be doing is beteen the fridge and your TV.

11-20 points: Armchair nomad

You have found your perfect place, and you feel at peace with your job. Vacations are fun, but you love returning home. You'd do best to spend your energy optimizing your current lifestyle. If you do choose to experiment with the digital nomad lifestyle, you'll prefer spending longer periods in one spot, allowing your destination to grow on you. And if this way of life still isn't for you, don't worry – your home is just a flight away.

21-30 points: Aspiring nomad

You'd love to explore the world, but some things are holding you back. In this guide, you will find inspiration and practical tips to help you jump those hurdles, whether it's friends and relatives, work, material possessions, or fear of the unknown. A good solution for you may be to take shorter trips while keeping your home base. But be warned: you might get addicted to the lifestyle.

31-40 points: Born nomad

You are a real citizen of the world. Not bound to one place, you feel at home wherever you are. You are not too attached to your belongings, and you don't mind being alone. When you do get together with others, you feel most at ease with other 'free spirits'. You may already live on the road. But if you are still 'stuck' in one country; now is the time to spread your wings. Yes, you're real digital nomad material!

Motivational speaker Esther Jacobs (1970), got 'fired' from her country for traveling too much. The Netherlands de-registered her, because her way of life 'did not fit the system', even though she owned a house, paid taxes, and ran her own business. Esther managed to turn this into an opportunity and is now an advocate of the digital nomad lifestyle. The Dutch government now even seeks her advice on the topic!

Originally from the Netherlands, I have always travelled a lot. Curiosity, a sense of adventure and a strong need to learn, guided my trips to over a 100 countries. I have been to places as diverse as Haiti, Transnistria (a non-existing country!), Madagascar, French Guiana, and Colombia. No matter where I travelled, however, after a few days, weeks or months, I always returned to the Netherlands.

In the past 5-10 years, my needs changed. I did not want to be on the road so much, or travel so fast anymore. Instead of trying to see it all, I preferred to stay longer in one place, to feel at home there, rather than a visitor. I alternated among a few locations I had grown fond of: my home near Amsterdam, my father's place in Miami, my ex-boyfriend's house on the Caribbean island of Curacao, and a small farm we were restoring in the heart of Mallorca. Still I was restless and was not able to stay in one place for more than six weeks at a time.

One day, when I went to get a new passport in the city hall in my hometown of Amstelveen, they refused to extend my passport. Apparently, there is a law that states you are only allowed to register in the Netherlands if you stay at least four months per year at one address. According to the government, I travelled too much. I was told that I could no longer use my address as my official residence. "But it is my own house!" I objected. "This is the only fixed-base that I have; I don't live anywhere else." My protests went all the way to the Minister of Internal Affairs, and later to the national media. But the rule was applied strictly. "We are sorry, this is the law. The system is just not fit for mobile citizens like you," was the final comment of the Dutch Government.

As a result, I was de-registered from my own house, I could not extend my passport, I lost my voting rights, and my right to social security, a pension, and all other privileges Dutch citizenship offers. I also got kicked out of their health insurance, without any alternative. For lack of an official address, my company could no longer be registered at the Chamber of Commerce, and I nearly lost my bank accounts and mobile phone number. The only official institute that still considered me a Dutch citizen was the IRS (Dutch Tax). They still wanted me to pay taxes!

That was the last push I needed to truly become a global citizen, PT or digital nomad, however you want to call it. I rented out my house to expats (providing me with a modest income), registered a company on the BVI (no taxes, so no need to keep track of expenses), and decided to focus on my opportunities instead of the limitations.

As a motivational speaker, I only need to be at a specific location when I am booked for a presentation. As an author, I can work from anywhere. All my archives are digital, so I always have access to my documents, pictures, etc. My website and social media can be updated from anywhere. As long as I have Wi-Fi, I can choose to be wherever I like; sometimes in a city, on a beach, in a spring-like climate or in a ski resort.

It takes patience and creativity, but there is a solution for everything. I found a way to renew my passport. There is a special 'window' for homeless people in the Netherlands. (Guess I am the only one with a house and company). And IKEA Family, in Spain, offers cheap worldwide health insurance, even if you are not a citizen of Spain.

www.estherjacobs.info

DESIGN YOUR OWN INTERNATIONAL MASTER PLAN & 'SIX FLAG THEORY'

Are you not completely happy with:
- ★ Your current work/life balance?
- ★ The mentality of the people around you?
- ★ The climate at your location?
- ★ The politics of your country?
- ★ The price level in your country?
- ★ The tax climate of your government?
- ★ The traffic?
- ★ The work ethics?
- ★ The amount of freedom or privacy you feel?
- ★ The (lack of) adventure in your life?

Then why don't you choose the countries or locations that fit best with your ideals? It doesn't have to be just one country or city; you can mix and match as you please, since your new life as a digital nomad is based on complete freedom. Literally anything is possible. Your life will definitely become more interesting, and possibly even cheaper. But in order for this to work long term, you need a smart strategy.

'SIX FLAG THEORY'

Not too long ago, 99% of people worked, lived, married, and eventually died, in the same country they were born. Apart from a few weeks of holidays or an occasional year abroad, most of a person's life was spent in that one country. Institutions and rules are based on this premise. Bank accounts, businesses, insurance, taxes, laws and regulations, all assume we have a 'home country' or 'place of permanent residence'.

But so many things have changed. Nowadays you can be born in country A, have a passport from country B, own a house in C, work in D, register your company in E, invest in F and host your websites in G, while you live in/travel to country H - Z. If you make smart, informed choices of what you do where, you can benefit in multiple ways.

The 'Flag Theory' calls to arrange different facets of your life to fall under the jurisdiction of separate countries or 'flags'. Most countries treat foreigners far better than their own citizens. PTs ('Perpetual Travelers', 'Permanent Tourists' or even 'Previous Taxpayers') structure their paperwork in a way that all governments regard them as tourist or traveler. The idea behind the original 'Three Flags Theory' by Harry Schultz, the 'Five Flags Theory' by W.G. Hill, and the more recent 'Six Flags Theory' by Bye Bye Big Brother, is that smart, freedom-seeking individuals should not be bound in their allegiances to just one government.

The strategy is to use different governments, or flags, for different parts of your life:

- ⭐ **Passport and citizenship** in a country that gives you optimal freedom to travel.
- ⭐ **Residency** in a country that does not tax money earned outside the country (tax haven). Note that this legal 'official' residence is not necessarily where you physically spend your time.
- ⭐ **Business haven** (where you earn your money): Base your business and speculations in stable countries, with low corporate tax rates.
- ⭐ **Asset haven** (where you keep your money): A money management or offshore banking center, ideally somewhere with low taxation of savings, interest, and capital gains.
- ⭐ **Playgrounds** (where you spend your money): live like a tourist in countries with low consumption tax, VAT, and low cost-of-living in general.
- ⭐ **Electronic haven in cyberspace**: a virtual country where your servers and websites are located. Ideally somewhere safe, with low regulation.

Reasons to structure your life along two or more flags

There can be various triggers or considerations to structure your life this way. Esther found out the hard way that many laws and regulations have not yet been updated to include digital nomad lifestyles. Many digital nomads pioneer in the field of (inter)national laws, which can sometimes get so tiring and difficult that 'stepping out of the system' seems the only option.

Others are motivated by adventure and/or price differences between different parts of the world. It is nowadays possible to make your money in euros or dollars and spend it in a country with a favorable exchange rate or lower cost-of-living, resulting in less need for work, and/or a more luxurious lifestyle (see page 83). Some seek adventure and variety; they need a change of scenery, want to travel, explore, meet new people, while discovering their own limits in the process. They consider the world to be their playground. (See PLAY page 260).

Another 'breed' of digital nomads is mainly lured by sovereignty. They desire a life with minimal (preferably zero) governmental interference. They achieve their ultimate freedom - self-ownership – by 'checking out of the system'. Privacy can be a concern, too; "Big Brother is watching you!" (Orwell, 1984). By traveling so much and living outside of the system, no government will have access to the full picture. Tax savings might also be a trigger; moving between countries on a regular basis may legally reduce or eliminate your tax burden. By lacking a legal, permanent residential status, some seek to avoid the legal obligations that may accompany residency, such as social security contributions, jury duty, and military service.

Yet others are seriously concerned about current events in the world, and are looking for economically and/or politically-resilient countries; locations that are better able to cope with the changes that are happening right now. Author Neil Strauss is one of these people. He started a search for a safe country to survive in case everything we know falls (further) apart "after the last few years of violence and terror, of ethnic and religious hatred, of tsunamis and hurricanes—and now of world financial meltdown." Strauss wrote the book Emergency about this journey of discovery.

EMERGENCY BY NEIL STRAUSS

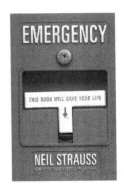

"Learn to be self-sufficient and survive without the system. I've started to look at the world through apocalypse eyes." As the economic downturn, continuing climate change, and the prevailing terrorist threat prove that the dangers facing our world loom larger than ever, Strauss decides he's had enough. But rather than watch helplessly, he decides to do something about it. Soon, he is investigating ways of getting second citizenship on the island of St. Kitts, protecting his assets offshore, and making friends with an elite group of billionaires who are thinking exactly the same thing.

With the same quick wit, and eye for cultural trends that marked The Game, The Dirt, and How to Make Love Like a Porn Star, Emergency traces Neil's white-knuckled journey through today's heart of darkness, as he sets out to move his life offshore, test his skills in the wild, and remake himself as a gun-toting, plane-flying, government-defying survivor. It's a tale of paranoid fantasies and crippling doubts, of shady lawyers and dangerous cult leaders, of billionaire gun nuts and survivalist superheroes, of weirdo's, heroes, and ordinary citizens going off the grid. It's one man's story of a dangerous world–and how to stay alive in it.

"Before the next disaster strikes, you're going to want to read this book. When The Shit Hits The Fan, it might just save your life. Because tomorrow doesn't come with a guarantee." (Strauss, 2009)

 bit.ly/neil-emergency

It may sound difficult, complicated, or expensive to design your own international master plan, but it is not. In the next chapters we'll give you some ideas and guidelines.

Most people don't want or need to become full-fledged PTs. Pick and choose what feels good to you, what fits your situation best. Just remember, every person, situation, and country is different, so interpret the information in your own way. You may even decide it makes more sense to stay registered in your own country and keep things they way they are. At least you'll have an idea of the alternatives. Also, we recommend you invest in an international tax consultant to make sure you're playing by the rules. And definitely get good legal advice, because laws differ a lot between countries and they change constantly. Usually it's good to keep things as simple as possible.

I) OPTIMIZE YOUR CITIZENSHIP AND PASSPORT FOR MAXIMUM FREEDOM

Most of us are citizens of the country where we were born, even though we may be residents somewhere else (more about residency on page 45).

A citizen is a person who is acknowledged as a legal member of a community, usually a nation. The citizenship is good for a lifetime and cannot be revoked unless there is substantial evidence of a crime against the state. Some of the main rights of a citizen are political rights, right to work, and access to education and health care. Widely known duties of a citizen of a state are payment of taxes and military service.

Learn more about the differences between citizenship and residency through the following link: **bit.ly/residency-citizenship**

A passport specifies your nationality, citizenship, and/or the place of residence. It is not just a travel document; it is also a certified proof of identity. A passport may or may not grant the right to a country's consulate/embassy protection.

HOW POWERFUL IS YOUR PASSPORT?
Some passports are easier to travel with than others. At the top of the list are the U.S. and the U.K., with easy-visa or visa-free access to 147 countries. Germany, South Korea, and France, are next, all with 145 countries apiece. Next are Italy and Sweden, at 144 nations each. It is no surprise that North Korea (44) and war-torn Iraq (38) score low. At the bottom of the Passport Index we find The Palestinian Territories in the Mideast, and Myanmar (Burma) in Southeast Asia, each with just 28 easy-travel destinations.

Find out how your passport ranks: **www.passportindex.org**

Source: bit.ly/passport-rankings

Most people have a passport (and citizenship) in the country they were born. Some people have dual passports, giving them the option to use the best passport for each purpose. If your passport is a powerful passport, you'll probably want to keep it, even if your residency changes to another country.

One of the reasons to obtain a different passport / citizenship may be that your passport is from a country that hinders your travel more than it facilitates it. Maybe you don't agree with the obligations that come with your citizenship (e.g. military service, jury duty, taxes). Or, for some reason, you don't have a passport. Citizenship of a country affords you the right to a passport.

There are four ways to obtain a citizenship:
* being born in a country
* marriage
* family relations
* naturalization

If you are exploring alternatives, keep these tips in mind:
* Prefer smaller countries with a good visa network.
* Check that there is no tax or military service for non-residents.
* Some passports can be obtained without residency; these have preference for digital nomads.
* Some options: Panama, Paraguay, Uruguay, Belgium, Brazil and Canada.

If you are really serious about becoming a PT, then your medium-term goal should be two or more citizenships.

PASSPORT ALTERNATIVES
Some countries and international organizations issue travel documents that are not standard passports, but enable the holder to travel internationally to countries that recognize the documents.

EU ID card
National identity cards are issued to citizens of all European Union member states (except Denmark, Ireland, and the United Kingdom), and to citizens of Liechtenstein and Switzerland (the latter not formally part of the EEA). These cards can be used as an identity document within their country of origin and also as a travel document within the EEA and Switzerland. National identity cards are often accepted for unofficial identification purposes (such as age verification in bars) in other parts of the world.
Source: bit.ly/identity-cards

Refugee passport
Stateless persons may be able to obtain a refugee travel document or Geneva passport, formerly called "Nansen passport". This document is issued by the state in which the refugee normally resides, and enables travel to countries that recognize the papers and sometimes to return to the issuing country.

World Passport

Everyone has the right to leave any country, including his own, and to return to his country.
– Article 13(2) of the Universal Declaration of Human Rights –

"If freedom of travel is one of the essential marks of the liberated human being, then the very acceptance of a national passport is the mark of the slave, serf or subject" explained Garry Davis, the initiator of the World Passport in 1948. "The very existence of the World Passport challenges the exclusive assumption of sovereignty of the nation-state system. It is designed to conform to nation-state requirements for travel documents. It does not, however, indicate the nationality of its bearer, only his or her birthplace. It is therefore a neutral, apolitical document of identity and potential travel document."

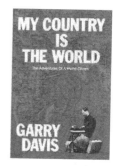

More than a million people have a World Passport. Either as refugees, because they had no other option, or as a Western protest against the system, or simply as a fun wanna-have. Anyone can request one at the World Government of World Citizens. It costs US $45 plus shipping (from the USA), and is valid for three years. Unfortunately, there is only a paper form (downloadable from the website), and the request can only be sent by mail, not (yet) over the internet.

 www.worldgovernment.com

The World Passport is officially recognized by only six countries: Burkina Faso, Ecuador, Mauritania, Tanzania, Togo and Zambia, although Immigration officials in many other countries have occasionally stamped or accepted one. Traveling with a World Passport may sound like an adventure, but in most cases will get you into a delay, trouble, or even prison. We think a World Passport is appropriate as either a fun trinket or if you really don't have any other passport. Unless, of course, your goal is to protest and/or learn more about bureaucracy. If you want to make a statement and are willing to engage in interesting discussions, then this might be your battle!

Garry Davis's adventures as the first world citizen traveling with his (home made) world passport, make a fascinating read:

 bit.ly/world-passport

2) STRATEGICALLY CHOOSE YOUR RESIDENCY

A residency permit grants you the legal right to live, work, travel, or study in a country, while still holding a foreign citizenship and passport. Your legal residence is not necessarily where you physically spend your time, but it is your official income tax residence. The residency is time-limited, and you have to conform to the rules and requirements in order to keep it valid; like having to spend a minimum amount of days per year in the country. Should you be convicted of a criminal offense, you could lose your status. As a permanent resident, you are not eligible to vote in federal or provincial elections.

Ideally, you would look for a country, residency permit or visa with:
- ✳ Favorable tax laws for earned income (capital gains and dividends are probably less relevant for digital nomads).
- ✳ Local bank account access to support the income
- ✳ Flat tax for a specific period of stay
- ✳ Protection by a bilateral tax agreement

These factors would be important to establish a proper residency flag, that could be recognized by your previous country of residency.

Once you have set up the residency and legal entity, you would have to spend the required minimum amount of days per year in that country in order to be considered a tax resident of that newly established residency flag. Then you could travel elsewhere as desired. Unfortunately, the 'perfect' country does not exist yet, so you have to figure out what works best for you. If taxation is your main worry, look for countries with territorial income tax and extensive Double Tax Agreements (DTA) networks.

DOUBLE TAX AGREEMENTS

If a business or individual who is resident in one country makes a taxable gain in another, they may be obliged by domestic laws to pay tax on that gain locally, and pay again in the country in which the gain was made.

Since this is unfair, many nations make bilateral double taxation agreements. In some cases, this requires that tax be paid in the country of residence and be exempt in the country in which it arises. In the remaining cases, the country where the gain arises deducts taxation at source (withholding tax) and the taxpayer receives a compensating foreign tax credit in the country of residence to reflect the fact that tax has already been paid. To do this, the taxpayer must declare himself to be non-resident in the 'foreign' country.

The second aspect of the agreement is that the two taxation authorities exchange information about such declarations, and so may investigate any anomalies that might indicate tax evasion. While individuals, or natural persons, can have only one residence at a time, corporate persons, owning foreign subsidiaries, can be simultaneously resident in multiple countries.

In the European Union, member states have concluded a multilateral agreement on information exchange. This means that they will each report (to their counterparts in each other's jurisdiction) a list of those savers who have claimed exemption from local taxation on the grounds of not being a resident of the state where the income arises.

Source: Wikipedia (bit.ly/double-tax)

IMMIGRATION BY INVESTMENT

Many of us were lucky enough to be born in developed countries, with access to visas and almost unhindered travel. This is a privilege few of us are aware of. What if you were born a developing nation with bad visa treaties and few travel options? We recently read a Facebook post of a guy from the occupied territories in Palestine. He had enjoyed a few months of living and traveling in Europe on his student visa. After graduating, he had to go back to his home country and was not able to get visa anymore. On Facebook he followed his fellow travelers, and became frustrated that his movements were much more restricted, simply because of where he was born. One of the ways for him (and others who feel they are hindered by their nationality) to travel more freely is to change nationalities, through investing in a country that allows for fast-track residency or citizenship.

Immigration by investment is a billion dollar industry, with non-transparent pricing and processes. Passports.io shows pricing of investment opportunities in different countries around the world that have official residency or citizenship by investment programs.

WHERE TO REGISTER?

Apparently, Panama is one of the easiest countries to get a permanent residency. You don't even have to live there. A Dutch nomad got her permanent residence visa within nine days. Also, if you are 55+, you are considered to be retired.

The Dominican Republic is another option. You are allowed to be gone for up to a year at a time, and still qualify as a resident.

 More on the Dominican Republic: **bit.ly/second-passport**

Other countries that are often mentioned are Malta ($$$), Malaysia ($$), and possibly the Philippines ($). Always check with an expert what specific rules apply in that country for your nationality.

European nationals can live and work in other EU countries. So instead of looking for a 'tropical' destination, it might be worth investigating other European countries, their rules and tax systems.

Estonia is often mentioned as a possible (e)residence, but this option is currently only attractive for companies (more info on page 56).

Unfortunately, it is not yet possible to become a resident of Estonia in such a way that it replaces your registration in another country. But the way things keep on developing, they might offer a service like this in the near future, so do keep an eye on e-Estonia.

bit.ly/e-residents

It might seem like a logical idea to register yourself as a resident in the country where you base your offshore company, to avoid problems with your home country's tax authorities. Beware however, that the characteristic of most offshore structures is that you are not allowed to do business in the country where your offshore company is based, hence the name 'offshore'.

It might be the best to build your life in the country where you (want to) spend most of your time (later).

DILEMMA: TO BE REGISTERED OR NOT?

Although we are led to believe the opposite, you don't have to be registered anywhere to live, work, and play. Many people find this a scary thought, but Esther can tell from experience that the sun still rises and sets every day, whether you are officially registered or not. That said, it does make life a lot easier to be registered as a resident in some place.

Esther experienced first-hand that most officials just don't understand the concept of 'not living in one place'. Each time you enter a country, for example, you have to give your 'home address' to immigration officials. Leaving that section blank will get you into trouble. By writing down just any address, they will let you pass without question, but you are, in fact, committing fraud by doing so. If, however, you try to explain your situation, they quickly transfer you to a small room for 'difficult cases', after which you are lucky to be let into the country a few hours later by finally producing that fraudulent 'home address'.

We deregistered from The Netherlands in 1997, but found that it is difficult to be 100% nomadic. We tried it as an experiment. We traveled all over the world for a year with only one large suitcase each. We stayed in hotels, serviced apartments, and lived on our boat. We liked it! But we have come to the conclusion that even though we no not need a fixed base, the rest of the world wants us to have one. Especially banks, insurance companies, governments, and tax authorities just don't get it. So we have chosen Luxembourg as a European base and Singapore as an Asian base. These countries are very business-minded, and they tolerate nomadic portfolio careerists.
— Abel and Adrienne —

Tax authorities also pose a problem; they are reluctant to accept that a person has officially left the country if the person can't produce an address they have moved to. If that section in their system remains blank, it is cause for distrust and thus, investigation. After two years without an official residence, Esther finally capitulated and registered in Mallorca, Spain. By providing her 'new address', many old problems seemed to be solved and new problems avoided.

You'd be surprised how many things are linked to residency:
* Voting (local, national, European level).
* Social security and other government provisions.
* Health insurance (in some countries provided for free to residents, others might have a special subsidized residents rate).
* Access to and use of government systems with a special password (DigID in The Netherlands, etc.).
* Pension (both adding to the provision, and the right to receive it).
* Taxes (personal, income, wealth, car, real estate, business etc.).
* Duties like military service, jury duty, etc.
* Getting a mortgage or personal loan.
* In some countries (e.g. the Netherlands) homeowners can deduct mortgage payments from their taxes only if they are residents of that country.
* Parking permits.
* Registering a company in the Chamber of Commerce (sole proprietorship is linked to a person who has to be a resident. Incorporation is different, which can often be achieved without residency; more about this on page 215).
* Deduction of VAT.
* Opening a bank account.
* Getting married.
* Registering the birth of a baby.
* Registering a death. If a person is not registered anywhere, they cannot be removed from the register after they die. Officials find that very troubling. ;)

What are your options?

1) Stay registered in your home country. This is familiar territory; you know both the rights and obligations.

2) Move to another country. You could actually physically live there, or just register on paper. Strategically, choose a country with favorable terms and taxes.

3) De-register from your home country and don't register anywhere else.

4) Register as a 'sojourner'; this means your home country knows that you are traveling and other countries know you are just passing through. Apparently, it is internationally accepted to be a sojourner for two years. After that, you have to register somewhere for a while, before you can go for another two years of sojourning. Some countries have a system to register nationals who travel overseas. The Netherlands, for example, has the RNI (Register Niet Ingezetenen). Other locations register incoming sojourners, like Florida's Sojourner's permit for boat owners who reside for more than 90 days. Most countries have no special registration system for sojourners.

Advantages of residence:

* No hassle at airports and with officials in general.
* Registration makes many things easier: insurance, obtaining passports and other papers, bank accounts, phone plans, renting houses, schooling your kids, buying a car, etc.
* In some countries you have a right to social security, pension, and other benefits.
* If anything happens to you, 'the system' takes care of you (depending on where you are registered).

Disadvantages of residence:

* Registration means administration, filling out forms, giving information to authorities, and often also obligates you to pay taxes.
* You have to live by the rules of the country you are registered. Laws might even limit the number of months you are 'allowed' to travel.
* You are traceable, expected to reply to letters of officials, and are liable to fines if you don't.

ACTING LEGALLY CORRECT WITHOUT REGISTRATION

When you enter a country, you always have to provide your permanent residence address. Leave that section blank, and you're in trouble. If you give an address where you are not officially registered, you are committing a crime. To avoid this, you should specify your last known official address; for example, the last hotel you stayed at. This is officially a temporary - so a legally correct - address.

TAXES

When you live in a country and/or receive benefits, it's only fair that you contribute by paying taxes. If you move from one country to another, your tax duties might shift to the other country. It depends if the two countries have a mutual tax ruling. So always ask an expert for advice.

But what if you don't live in a specific country? There is no clear tax law for digital nomads.

Chances are, the tax service in your country of birth doesn't want to let you go. They will claim that you still have to pay taxes on your world income. You can either abide, or fight that decision. Or you can find a smart solution, such as reducing your world income, having more deductible expenses to lower your income, leading revenue streams through an international (trust) company, or registering in a tax-friendly country.

It is important to keep in mind that the 'game' is NOT to avoid taxes, but to find a system that is fair to both you(r company) and the facilities (public spaces, infrastructure etc.) that you use.

Of course each country, law and situation is different, but in general (inter)national tax law has the following principles. A citizen needs to pay tax in their home country over their world income. So if you are registered in Germany and make money in Hong Kong, the German tax service can and will tax you.

There are a few exceptions:
* Some countries specify the number of days you have to be there in order to have a tax obligation. This differs greatly per country. You find some examples on page 64. This means that if as a German citizen, for example, you spend less than 183 days in Germany, you probably don't have to pay taxes. The USA has a different rule: when you were born in the USA you always have to pay taxes there. Even if you have not set foot in the country for 30 years!
* There are exceptions for double tax payments.
Countries that have DTA (double tax agreements) respect the fact that if you pay tax in another country, that you don't have to pay tax in your country of origin, or only have to pay the difference.

Rob Greenfield is an American adventurer, environmental activist, and an entrepreneur on a mission to entertain, educate, inspire, and give back to the world. He traveled through the USA without a penny. He shares his interesting view on taxes.

IS IT OK TO NOT PAY TAXES?

Some would argue that if you are not spending money and you aren't paying taxes, you are mooching from public systems such as the roads, parks, and libraries. That could hold true but you can assure that not to be the case by living in service of your country. And heck no I'm not talking about the army. I am talking about doing your part to help these systems that you are involved in but not paying taxes to do so.

- ✴ If you use the library, volunteer at it.
- ✴ If you use the public parks, clean up some trash.
- ✴ If you use the public bathrooms, leave them cleaner than you found them.

It's important to realize that reciprocation does not have to occur on a direct give and take basis. For example, a man could spend one hundred percent of his money, say 1 million dollars, on creating a safe highway infrastructure for Americans but does that mean that he doesn't deserve to use the public parks, the library, or walk down the sidewalk? Of course not.

Maybe you don't have a way to give back to the road system but you could dedicate time to getting more people to walk, lessening the impact on the roads. Maybe you don't pay for health care but you can keep others that use free health care out of the hospitals by teaching them to be healthier via their eating and exercise habits. In these ways you can actually save taxpayers money, which would cover

your lack of financial contribution. It's important to note that 50% of taxes go to war so when you do pay taxes you are funding war.
You have to think outside the box to understand this but taxes are by no means the only way to contribute. Money is not the only form of transaction, although we have been led to believe that.

You can be a contributing member to society without paying taxes or using money. In fact you can contribute much more in this manner than you would by paying taxes. Once you realize this, your possibilities are endless and the future ahead of you will shine bright.

bit.ly/rob-greenfield

3) FIND A BUSINESS HAVEN THAT FITS YOUR NEEDS

Even if you don't live in one place, you will need somewhere to send your invoices from. That location is where you officially make the money you earn, so you better choose it wisely. Base your business (where you earn your money) in stable countries, with low corporate tax rates. Depending on the line of business you are in, also consider territorial tax, subsidies, labor costs, reliable legal system, and/or privacy.

Esther chose to incorporate her business in the British Virgin Islands (BVI). It was easy to set up, the yearly fee is low, and she has no obligation to pay taxes or do extensive bookkeeping. Ducat-trust.com in Curaçao arranged everything for her. Esther uses her own name as a company name, and is very transparent about why and how she set up her company this way. The freedom she feels with this 'no strings attached' form of incorporation puts a smile on her face every day.

Apart from the BVI, other options are: Delaware, UK, HK, Singapore, Dubai, RAK, Nevis and the Marshall Islands.

Offshore companies are often regarded as 'suspicious' and your home country's tax service might give you trouble, so do check with an expert.

Unfortunately, there is no 'one size fits all' solution, and each business has unique needs. Be sure to talk to a professional and understand the tax, legal, and financial ramifications that come with shareholding or directorship of a legal entity. More info in WORK page 215.

WHAT ABOUT E-ESTONIA?

The tiny European country of Estonia is one of the first to completely revolutionize the way government and citizens interact. Everything is digital and all systems are linked. Estonia switched completely from paper to digital, so communication with and by the government is via email, and electronic signatures are accepted. Their e-residency sounds very interesting for digital nomads. You can register your company in e-Estonia (online, and within a day!) and get an identification card, which allows worldwide official digital signing of documents. But is this the solution we are all looking for?

Edmund John Lowell, of incorporations.io, explains: "Many people are confused and think that Estonia e-residency is an actual right to reside. We should be clear that e-residency would NOT make you a resident for tax purposes. Personal taxation and corporate taxation are different matters. The program is a fantastic, entrepreneurial initiative. A very savvy move to attract foreign direct investment and open up bank accounts remotely while providing KYC/AML compliance on a internationally tolerable level."

More info on: **bit.ly/e-residents**
or watch the video on: **bit.ly/e-estonia-docu**

Co-author André Gussekloo (1980) and his girlfriend Marta took their laptops and their cat on a trip to Thailand. The experiment proved successful, so they also traveled through Central America. They now live on Lanzarote with their baby boy, but still like to escape for a few months a year.

I met my Spanish girlfriend —Marta— when I hitchhiked through Europe in 2004. In 2006 we fell for a well-paid job at Shell's IT Helpdesk in Manchester (UK). There I realized I wasn't wired to work for a boss and started looking for a way out. Since I always loved writing, becoming a freelance copywriter seemed the most logical step. When Marta decided to pursue a Masters degree in the Canary Islands, I decided to take the plunge.

SEO copywriting turned out to be (and still is) a good way to make money remotely. When I began looking for writing gigs in 2006 I used the freelancer marketplaces. Then when I had some experience and some references to show for it, I cold emailed internet marketing agencies, which got me more and better paid work. Nowadays I don't have to hunt clients down; they find me through Google, which is proof that my search engine optimization (SEO) efforts are successful.

We spent the year 2013 in Thailand and we were crazy enough to take our cat with us (see page 150). In 2014 we traveled from Costa Rica to Mexico overland, while the cat stayed with its grandparents in the Netherlands. It was great to be able to catch chicken buses and stay in places without having to mind a pet. The trip through Central America was rewarding in different ways: I did a 'live launch' of an e-course which I still enjoy income from, and we conceived our son Diego on the way.

While I first became a freelancer and then discovered that I could work from anywhere, I still think I should take advantage of my location independence. Before we had a child, I used to say "now is the time – we don't have kids or a mortgage yet". Turns out you can travel perfectly with a child, although priorities and activities change.

I have also dabbled in passive income systems, such as publishing e-books for the Amazon Kindle. I didn't write those myself, but outsourced them to ghostwriters and at one point I was up to $2,000 in royalties a month. With this book I am reigniting my self-publishing career.

Passive income didn't turn out to be all that passive. You need to work to maintain the system and sooner or later competitors will catch up. I'm convinced that freelancing is the best way to enjoy freedom – both from a boss and from the office. I now teach people who like writing how they can turn their hobby into a profitable, location-independent career with my course Beachwriter.net.

In the past years, the digital nomad scene has really exploded. I love to be in the midst of this revolution, where people are pushing the boundaries of what is normal and what is possible. On a deeper level, I think the digital nomad lifestyle can really help people see what's important in life and think about how you can make a more meaningful impact. As you can see in this guide, the digital nomad lifestyle ties in with so many interesting concepts: minimalism, travel hacking, the 'sharing economy', productivity, entrepreneurship, offshore companies, technology, globalization... I'm happy and grateful to be living in these times!

 www.andregussekloo.com

4) SAFELY LET YOUR ASSETS WORK FOR YOU

The asset flag seems less applicable to the typical digital nomad. On the other hand, you don't have to be a millionaire to have 'assets'. Some countries consider shares in a company, a bank/savings account, a pension or house as 'wealth', and tax accordingly, whether you are resident of the country or not.

For example, Esther has to pay 1.2% tax on the value of her house (minus the amount of her mortgage) in the Netherlands, even though she does not reside in the country anymore. However, the monthly rent she receives is tax-free and outweighs the taxes she has to pay. In Germany home ownership is not taxed, but any rent income it generates, is taxed.

In The Netherlands financial gifts from parents to children and even inheritances are taxed, in Germany they aren't. To make an informed decision, check what taxes/rules apply in your country. Get solid advice, since bank, tax, and privacy laws vary and change.

If this flag does apply to you, store your 'wealth' in a location with no capital gains tax, and a stable banking system. Popular 'flags' used to be: Switzerland, Austria and Luxembourg, but because of reduced privacy they have now been replaced by Hong Kong, Singapore, and even some US online brokers.

Just before this book was published, a treaty of 91 countries accepted the OECD common reporting standard. At the end of each year, your bank account details and real estate transactions in each of these countries will be made available to the tax service in your country of origin. This means that from now on, everything is transparent, while prior to this agreement, the secrecy of some countries might have made them more attractive.

5) PICK YOUR PLAYGROUDS

A 'playground' is any place where you spend time for pleasure. You can live as a tourist in countries with a low cost of living, and/or those that offer activities/adventures you would like to experience. You can choose locations with the quality of life and lifestyle you prefer; where what you esteem is valued, not outlawed.

You can take advantage of different price-levels to keep your average cost of living manageable. For example, if you spend one month in a more expensive place like London, you could live three months in Thailand to compensate.

Tax-wise, it is advisable to have at least four playgrounds. Spend a maximum of three months per year in one country to avoid being considered a resident, or having to pay taxes.

So where should you go? What can you do there? And why should those destinations be on your bucket list? You will find ideas and inspiration in the last section of this book: PLAY, page 260.

6) EXPLORE CYBERSPACE

The virtual realm has become a sixth 'flag'. Even though cyberspace seems independent from a location, there is always a place where you store your data, place your server, and/or host your websites.

When considering where to locate your server, take the following factors into account:

* Quality of the infrastructure; varies greatly from country to country.
* Quality of the hosting providers available.
* Check reviews for good hosting providers: bit.ly/hosting-reviews or webhostinggeeks.com
* Or ask the following questions: How can you contact them and when? Do they make a daily backup of your site? Do they check their servers (with your sites) for malware or other vulnerabilities? Do they use a firewall to block cyber threats?
* Their connection to the global communications network.
* Safety, privacy, and regulations.
* Depending on your business and need for security you can choose Virtual Private Server (VPS) hosting (safer but more expensive), or shared hosting servers, leaving you more vulnerable to attacks by hackers, meaning you will have to check your site more often for malware. Check out this overview of data protection policies in the world: bit.ly/data-protection-handbook.
* Energy supply and reliability of the location of your servers.
* Proximity to your target markets. Select your hosting company preferably in the same country as where your (potential) customers are, as this can impact the search results in Google (or other search engines).
* Legal, political, environmental, and exchange risks. Maybe you even want to take climate change effects into account: bit.ly/survive-climate-change.

You can find the full checklist on: bit.ly/choose-hosting-location

The five best countries to locate your server (website data privacy):
- ★ Iceland
- ★ Norway
- ★ Netherlands
- ★ Switzerland
- ★ Romania

Motivation and more details can be found on: bit.ly/website-data-privacy

> *Even if you're not doing anything wrong, you are being watched and recorded.*
>
> Edward Snowden

BIG BROTHER IS WATCHING

Keep in mind that your domain name (for example, generic URLs like .com or .tv or .org, or country-specific ones like .es .nl .fr) not only means something to your clients, but can also provide information to government organizations and tax authorities. If your visa does not allow you to work from Indonesia, for example, they might argue that you do work from that location if you host your servers there. Or if you claim to have left your home country Germany, for example, but the domain name of your website is still www.xxx. de, the German tax authority might argue that you still have to pay taxes, because they see your website as 'roots' in Germany. Esther even had this argument with the Dutch tax authorities for having a website (www.estherjacobs.info), which may not have a country-specific top-level domain, but is partly in the Dutch language...

SOURCES AND MORE INFO ON SIX FLAG THEORY

* **Flagtheory.com** answers FAQ about the different flags – from residency to digital assets.
* **Nomadcapitalist.com** is a consultancy with a podcast and blog about living and doing business internationally. It is aimed at entrepreneurs who make at least $ 100,000 a year.
* **Streber.st** reviews bank, shines a spotlight on offshore jurisdictions and answers frequent questions about tax havens.
* The article at **bit.ly/five-flag** explores what applying the Five Flag or Six Flag theory would look like in real life.
* The Survival Podcast forum **(thesurvivalpodcast.com/forum)** is a discussion board for doomsday preppers, some of whom are five flag proponents.
* **Incorporations.IO** - by Edmund John Lowell, who also helped us with this section. Comparison and quantification of incorporation across different legal entities in various regions worldwide.
* Ronald Oenema, accountant and tax advisor for Dutch digital nomads: **ronaldoenema@virtus-online.nl**
* Ronald Kandelhard, German attorney and digital nomad specialist: **kandelhard@okb-anwalt.de**
* More in the WORK section of this book

COUNTRY SPECIFIC LEGAL AND TAX INFORMATION

It is possible for a non-national to live for several months in various different countries, and in some cases even own property, without becoming a legal tax resident, and therefore eliminating paying income tax.

The information below is a mix of bits and pieces very basic legal information and some indications of personal and corporate tax. It is purely an indication of how varied laws and regulations can be.

The list is composed of information we got from various digital nomads and found on Wikipedia. Please use it for orientation only: it is not legally specific and not complete.

Get professional tax advice before making a decision. Even within a country, laws are sometimes applied differently as well, as Esther experienced in the Netherlands (page34).

EUROPE

Most European countries allow tourists to spend up to three months (in some cases six months) in the country without being considered a resident or being required to file a local tax claim.

The Netherlands

* Residents have to spend a minimum of four months at an address to be eligible for registration and linked benefits, such as health insurance, social security, etc. It is very hard to prove to the tax service that you have really left the country. It seems they only accept tax payment in another country as sufficient proof.

* Foreigners spending more than eight months a year in The Netherlands are obliged to apply for residence.

* Are you a programmer or do you do work that can be paid in royalties? Then the Netherlands might be a good location for your company. For Dutch limited companies (BV) royalties are tax exempt. Meaning that you don't have to pay taxes on royalties received for your software, music or concept. Big corporations like Starbucks have based their European head office in The

Netherlands exactly for this reason. If you think this might apply to you, ask a tax advisor about the 'Dutch-Irish sandwich'.

- ★ Personal income tax: 33.5% -52%, including social security payments.
- ★ Corporate tax: 20.0% for the first €275,000 and above that a corporate tax rate of 25.5%.

Belgium
- ★ Non-residents can spend up to six months a year in the country, without having to pay taxes.
- ★ Income tax: 25-50%.
- ★ Corporate tax: 34%.

Spain
- ★ Non-residents can spend up to six months a year in the country, without having to pay taxes.
- ★ Personal income tax: 20-49%.
- ★ Corporate tax will be reduced to 25% in 2016. There is a lower tax rate for newly formed companies: 15% for the first two years in which the company obtains taxable profit.
- ★ Profits for freelancers ('autonomo') up to €20,000 a year are not taxed. The first tax bracket above that amount is 20%. However much or little you make, monthly payments to social security remain at the same relatively high level: €264 per month.

Germany
- ★ Non-residents can spend up to six months a year in the country, without having to pay taxes.
- ★ Residents spending more than 183 days a year abroad are tax exempt.
- ★ Income tax 14-45% plus 5,5% social security premiums.
- ★ Freelancers are not taxed over the first €8,000 they make. Profits that go over €8,000 are taxed between 14% and 45%. This may seem little, but freelancers are obliged to get a medical insurance. If a cheaper, private insurance does not accept them, they have to rely on the State insurance, which costs €360 a month.

Austria
* Non-residents can spend up to six months a year in the country, without having to pay taxes.
* Residents spending more than 183 days a year abroad are tax exempt.
* Personal income tax is 21-50%.
* Corporate tax is 25%.

United Kingdom
* Personal income 10-45%.
* Your first £ 10,000 are untaxed. The tax brackets above that vary from 10% to 45%. As for National Insurance contributions, the self-employed generally pay £2.75 a week, plus 9% on annual profits between £7,956 and £41,865. For income above that level, another 2% is added.
* Corporate tax: 20%.

Bulgaria
* Both personal income and corporate income are taxed at a flat rate of 10%. What's more, the costs of living are low and the internet speeds are high. With ski resorts for winter fun and beaches to hit in summer, Bulgaria might just become a new digital nomad playground.

The Czech republic
* Income taxes in Czech Republic are levied at a flat rate of 15% on gross income. Corporate tax rate in 2014 was 19%. One nomad explained that the first 60% of your income is tax free, the remaining 40% are taxed, resulting in a very acceptable percentage. The Czech republic is thinking of changing this rule, so do check!

Estonia

* Personal income tax: 20%.
* Corporate tax: 20%. However, Estonia knows a unique system, which shifts the moment of corporate taxation from the moment of earning the profits to the moment of their distribution. "In other words, earning profits in itself does not bring income tax liability, which arises only when earned profit is distributed to shareholders. In case profit distributed to shareholders originates from dividends received from subsidiary company or from permanent establishment corporation has in other country, then profit distribution is tax exempt." Source: bit.ly/estonia-tax.

REST OF THE WORLD
United States

* It is possible to spend up to 122 days each year in the United States without being considered a resident--or being required to file a US tax return. This applies only to non-US citizens who are not permanent residents and earn no income in the United States.
* The United States are special, because it's one of the few countries that taxes its non-resident citizens (even US nationals who haven't set foot in the US for decades). Some US billionaires have actually renounced their citizenship, in order to escape this stranglehold.
* US nationals: consult IRS publication #54 to stay up to-date on longer-term tax obligations. Think about where you will be based, and look into FEIE - the foreign earned income exclusion, which one can qualify for as either a bona fide resident, or via the physical presence test, which is essentially 330 days outside the US each year.
* The tax system for the self-employed is rather complicated. The minimum profit tax is 15.3%. There are all kinds of mitigating circumstances, like deductions, other income sources, whether or not you also have a part-time employed job, etc.

Canada

* Canada considers anyone spending 183 days or more per year to be a resident, for tax purposes.
* "Canadian residents and corporations pay income taxes based on their world-wide income. Canadians are in principle protected against double taxation receiving income from certain countries, which gave agreements with Canada through the foreign tax credit, which allows taxpayers to deduct from their Canadian income tax otherwise payable from the income tax paid in other countries. A citizen who is currently not a resident of Canada may petition the CRA to change her or his status so that income from outside Canada is not taxed." Source: bit.ly/canada-tax.
* Where income is earned in the form of a capital gain, only half of the gain is included in income for tax purposes; the other half is not taxed.
* Personal income tax: 15 – 29%.
* Corporate tax: federal 11-15%; special low rates for small companies, varying per state.

Australia

* Tax starts at the 19% level on income above $18,200. Once your profit rises above $37,000, the calculation gets complicated. A sample calculation can be found on the ASIC website. Suffice to say that taxes are pretty high once you start earning well.
* Corporate tax: 30%.
* A Working Holiday Visa allows you to work a maximum of six months for the same employer. After that, you can continue living in Australia on a Bridging Visa (a temporary visa that allows you to stay in Australia until further notice about the visa you are applying for). It is not well known that from the moment you get your Bridging Visa, you are allowed to work another six months for any company. Read the experience of surfer Lars Zeekaf: bit.ly/oz-visa-story

Panama

- ★ Personal income tax 7- 27%.
- ★ Corporate tax: 12% (profit) or 25% (statutory).
- ★ Regardless of your residency status, the tax is only applied to Panamanian-sourced income. So income outside of Panama is not taxed.
- ★ Virtually anyone can become a resident in Panama, since the application process is short and easy. Also, you are not required to be in Panama a minimum amount of days a year in order to hold on to your residency. You could be traveling around Asia while paying your tax in Panama (which is no tax if your clients are outside Panama).

Hong Kong

- ★ A Limited Company can be set-up by non-residents. Hong Kong does not have the suspicious tax haven image that countries like Belize and the Seychelles have. Income made outside Hong Kong is not taxed, but annual maintenance costs of the company are around US$2,000.

British Virgin Islands (BVI)

- ★ Esther has incorporated here. She does not have to pay tax, meaning she does not have to keep receipts, file reports, etc. You officially have to keep a record of the invoices you sent, but nobody is ever going to ask for them. The BVI have no tax agreements with The Netherlands, so the Dutch tax authorities might not recognize Esther's (none-) tax payment....

Freelance translator Martina Russo (1989) from Italy worked from the Galapagos Islands and other unusual places. She loves to immerse herself in nature and likes to do extreme sports wherever she travels.

I've always wanted (and needed) to be independent, so I started working when I was 16. Bars, restaurants, offices, exhibitions — all the way up to being an airline employee here in Milan, Italy, my hometown. It was a great job. I got to speak five languages each day, help out people, it felt like 'traveling' and, most importantly, I got free tickets to fly all over the world: Can you imagine flying from Italy to the States with €60 round trip?

At the same time, I was also attending university classes at the faculty of interpreting and translating. Attendance was mandatory and life was really hard: get up at 3 am, get into the uniform, drive to work as fast as you can, deal with freaked out crowds of passengers that forget what their name is as soon as they step into the airport, try not to send their bags to Beijing instead of Tokyo (oops!) and then rush to university, attend classes and take exams I'd be studying for between one flight and the other behind the check-in desk.

My bosses were horrible and money sucked. So one day I woke up and decided that I couldn't be 22 and have a nervous breakdown. I just packed up and left. I didn't really think about it too much. I just did it. That's when the idea of staying back home began to stink, so I started moving around.

At first I was working my ass off in restaurants and going back home every few months to take 25 exams within two weeks. But during my airport days, I had already landed my first translation client and was doing a bit of translating on the side. I started focusing on my translation business and really dived deep into it. I made a first attempt at creating a 'professional website' and a terrible CV. I started to apply with translation agencies and got the first (horribly) paid jobs. But no one told me how those things work, so I had to learn it the hard way.

During that time, I was living in a town on the Garda lake (North Italy) for the summer with my boyfriend at the time, and at some point we just took off to South East Asia. Then, money was just enough to get by, but my business was starting to take shape.

It's been a couple of years since then, and many more countries I've lived in or traveled to: Peru, Ecuador (the Galapagos islands!), Bosnia and Herzegovina, Croatia, Malta, Portugal, Italy (including a full winter season in the Alps, snowboarding!), Germany, Switzerland, Thailand, Cambodia, Laos; Austria, Liechtenstein, the Netherlands, the United States and whatnot. And I'm just about to move to Spain!

So, if you asked me: I love my life - even though sometimes it's very tough and stressful - and would rather jump off a cliff (this time not for sports) than going to back to work for someone else.

My work/office gear I usually carry around - and rarely exceed, otherwise my backpack gets too heavy:
- 2 smartphones (1 with local SIM card I buy when I get there to take on interpreting calls, and the other one with my Italian SIM card, so I can always check if clients are trying to reach me)
- Modem for portable Wi-Fi
- Portable battery for electronic devices
- My MacBook Air
- iPod & Kindle

Working on the road makes me feel motivated, but it has its challenges. Time zones, for one. Being in Thailand (+6 compared to Europe) works like a charm, but anywhere in the US/South America and that side of the world turns out to be fairly stressful — at least for someone who works mainly with European clients. I managed to get around it letting my ongoing clients know that I was abroad and they suited their schedule accordingly.

If I must be brutally honest, the 'hype' of the digital nomad doesn't particularly excite me. Many people are getting the idea that they should do a job they don't like and just get some money so they can travel to be the cool 'digital nomad' kids. I think it (should) work the other way around: you do something you love, you get really good at it, charge proper money for it and then set off to travel.

Anyhow, it looks like more and more people are 'joining the movement' and I've already seen an increase in products and services, specifically for the modern wanderer. Starting from hotels that turn into coworking/coliving spaces, guides and books, apps, devices and so on. I'm not sure where it's headed, but it's certainly setting new standards and making this way of living more acceptable in the eyes of companies, and society in general. All good things!

 movingwordstranslations.com

all
you
need
is
less

Most of us have an abundance of work, stress, to-do items, and stuff we hardly use. On the other hand, we all feel short on time, fun, peace and quiet, money and freedom to do what we really want. What if you could trade one for the other? Less work for more time? Less stuff for more freedom? Less stress for more fun? The good news is that you CAN. And you don't have to win the lottery or wait until your retirement.

Even if you don't want to become a digital nomad, minimizing will give you more space to focus on what you feel is really important. You can do this by changing how you spend your scarce resources, like time, money, and energy.

* By reducing your expenses, you need to work/earn less.
* If you get rid of most of your stuff (clothes, books, pictures, furniture, gadgets etc.), you'll have less to drag around, store, insure, protect, and worry about. Less stuff means more freedom.
* By finding out what work tasks you can STOP doing, automating part of your work, and outsourcing what is left, you create time to spend on things you really like.

Minimizing means making deliberate choices. In the next chapters, we share the choices we have made and the tips we received from declutter experts:

★ Reduce your expenses.
★ Declutter your world.
★ Tips to minimize your workload, you'll find in WORK, page 226.

Work and personal may get intertwined a little, but that is the result of the blurring line between the two.

Once you start decluttering, it might become a game, or even an addiction to reduce your expenses, stuff, and work, even more, in exchange for more freedom. How far will you go?

MORE WEALTH, MORE FREEDOM.
Seven tips to become less dependant on an income.

Wealth is a relative idea. It can be measured in absolute quantities, like how many times you can go on holiday to exotic locations, or how many yachts you can buy. But you can also consider the quality of your life. How much leisure time do you have, how happy can you be, how healthy? Look at the quality of your relationships, how much pleasure and fulfillment you get out of life. The first quantitative form of wealth is the one most of us were traditionally chasing. More stuff, better stuff; impress others. The second form is the one that was usually reserved for hippies and the like: less money, more quality. A better life, with more meaning.

Thanks to technology, we now have access to a hybrid form of wealth, combining luxury with meaning, which offers more quality, in all aspects of life, at a lower cost. Sustainable techniques, the availability of knowledge through the internet, the combination of many gadgets on one affordable smartphone, and the connectivity and creativity of millions of people. Add some willpower and it's easier than ever to become less dependent on your job, and create more freedom to design your life any way you want.

We offer seven tips to get you started:

1) Reduce your economical footprint (The less money you need, the less dependent you become).
2) Become a chronic minimalist (Make structural changes).
3) Train your happiness (Learn to enjoy small things).
4) Live really healthy (as opposed to 'marketing healthy', cook your own, unprocessed food).
5) Save money with your savings account (When you have a buffer for unexpected expenses, you don't need to insure them).
6) Work on becoming self-sustainable (Learn from others and share your experiences).
7) Nourish yourself on freedom (Less work, less money, more time, more freedom).

REDUCE YOUR EXPENSES

Instead of saving money beforehand so you can maintain your current spending level on your trip, a more sustainable idea is to create a habit and permanently reduce your expenses. That leaves room for working less, saving up more, or living like a king or queen at a cheaper destination.

The next chapters will give you practical, step-by-step tips to minimize your expenses (before and during your trip).

1) Reduce your fixed costs, become less dependent on an income
2) Don't spend money unnecessarily. Choose what you find important. Invest in experiences, not stuff.
3) Try to earn your income in a strong currency, such as euros or dollars.
4) Find a location where the cost of living is lower so your money lasts longer.
5) Try bartering, sharing and using the sharing economy.
6) Travel smarter and cheaper.

EXPERIMENT: LOG YOUR EXPENSES

Being aware of what you spend also makes you more conscious of how little you actually need.

Keep a log of your expenses (both business and private) for a month. Write down your expenses for housing, food, entertainment, transport, subscriptions, everything.

You could use this handy app: thebirdy.com

At the end of the month go through your log. What catches your eye? Are there any expenses that would be easy to cut or reduce? Anything you would not miss at all?

1) REDUCE YOUR FIXED COSTS

Most of us are used to paying rent, monthly utility bills, insurance, a car, TV, etc. What if you could reduce these dramatically?

Reduced expenses take a lot of pressure from your budget. If you can cut your monthly or yearly fixed expenses, you can work less and feel more freedom, more flexibility.

What is your biggest expense? We guess it is probably housing. Check page 111 on how you can eliminate or reduce those costs, or maybe even make money from your place!

Zoe Melnik gives detailed examples from her own experience and explains why travelling permanently through Europe is cheaper than the 9-to-5 life she had in Toronto. She takes rent, food, transportation, and additional bills into consideration:

 bit.ly/traveling-europe

Some tips to live on less money, whether you are already traveling, or still in the preparation phase:

🟆 Do you still own a car? Do you really need it? You could either sell it and use public transportation, use a bike, share somebody else's car, or rent out your car when you are not using it, through one of the many car-sharing platforms like:

 RelayRides.com, bit.ly/hire-your-car, Snappcar.com, Zipcar.com.

🟆 Review your subscriptions and cancel all or most of them. Who needs newspapers, magazines, etc., when you can get all info online for free? Instead of going to the gym, practice indoor or outside. You could even cancel your internet plan and only go online for free at a Wi-Fi cafe or hotspot.

- Revise your insurance portfolio. Do you need all of those policies? Are they still applicable for your new lifestyle? Often there are more suitable or cheaper versions available. Sometimes you get a discount if you put them all with one agent. An alternative to insurance is to save some money to build your own buffer, in case anything unexpected happens.
- Check your phone plan. What part of your bill consists of monthly recurring costs? Is it a suitable plan to use abroad? Cancel your expensive phone plan in time, before it is automatically renewed for another year. You'll find alternatives on page 132.
- Alcohol and tobacco are expensive in most countries. If you have wanted to quit for a while, this may be your moment. Imagine all the (healthy) things you could do with the money saved.

2) CHOOSE HOW YOU SPEND YOUR MONEY

Only spend money on what you find important. Most likely this will mean, invest in experiences, not stuff.

Start practicing this new way of (not) spending money while you are still in your home country. Some tips and choices that might help:

- Do you regularly get coffee at a Starbucks or similar popular coffee places? What if you chose to spend those €5 (or 10 or 20) per week on something else? That would save you €260/ €520 / €1040 per year; that is a flight to an exotic destination!
- Instead of buying expensive gifts, you could make them yourself. Esther sometimes paints the name of a newborn baby on a piece of driftwood as an original and personal present to the new parents. Friends would also appreciate a voucher to take care of their kids for an evening. That way they could have some quality time together and you get to know their kids.

* Instead of going out for dinner, you could stay at home and cook for/with your friends. If you do go out, even the most expensive restaurants have affordable options on the menu. Alcohol is what usually drives up any bill. If your friends are not budget-minded, explain beforehand that you are saving up for a trip and offer to pay only for what you consume, instead of splitting the bill.

* Sometimes it's easier to hang out with like-minded people instead of friends who don't (need/want to) think about the money they spend. Use apps like Meetup.com, Nomadlist.com and Facebook events, and check the events calendar of the location you are visiting.

ESTHER'S CHOICES

* I looked at what's really important to me: communication. As a student, I decided that my telephone and travel expenses should never be an obstacle to doing what I wanted. This still applies to everything I do, both private and business. Call someone, go somewhere? The expenses are never an excuse for me to say "no".

* My biggest expense is plane tickets. Every euro I spend on a plane ticket, to me, is well spent. Still, it helps to compare prices and be flexible in your travel dates (more info on page 88). Once I arrive somewhere, I always live very frugally. I stay with friends or rent a simple room or apartment through Airbnb.com. But to get to a place, you occasionally have to spend some money.

* I collect experiences, instead of material things or money. Clothing, makeup, furniture, CDs, magazines, and other 'luxury items' don't appeal to me. I try to resist the temptation to buy stuff. When walking in a shopping area, I notice that I'm automatically attracted to the stores. The whole atmosphere says, 'Buy this,' or 'You really need that'. As a precaution, I don't go shopping, unless I really need something. If I feel an irresistible urge to buy something, I always sleep on it for a night or two. If I still want it, I buy it, but most of the time the urge has passed by then. How much do you spend on impulse buying?

My plea is not for frugal living, but to make clear choices for what you find important.

---

3) EARN YOUR INCOME IN A STRONG CURRENCY

If you earn your income in a relatively strong currency, for example in euros or dollars, this provides you more buying power in countries with less stable currencies. By remotely working in Europe or the US, and living in South America or Asia, for example, you get the most value for money.

Earning and saving some euros or dollars also provides you with a 'way out', if needed. When you earn in the local currency, airplane tickets might seem unreasonably expensive. Also, in an emergency situation local currencies don't always buy you airplane tickets, hospital care or an alternative.

The most important question remains not whether, but HOW, you can earn euros or dollars remotely. The WORK part of this book (starting on page 172) will give you some ideas and tips, while various digital nomads share their success stories throughout this book.

4) FIND A LOCATION WITH LOW COSTS OF LIVING

Many people think that traveling or living abroad is expensive. They don't realize that leaving your home country can actually be more economical than staying there, especially if you spend your money in a country or area where the cost of living is much lower.

Cheapest and most expensive countries to live in

A better life for half the price? It is very well possible. Cost of living varies greatly across continents, among countries and even cities/villages (see bit.ly/cost-of-living-2016). The following areas are often mentioned as cheapest countries to live:

- ✵ Southern and Eastern Europe (e.g. Hungary, Romania, Greece, Spain and Portugal)
- ✵ Central and South America (e.g. Panama, Brazil, Guatemala, Peru and Belize)
- ✵ Asia (e.g. India, Nepal and Indonesia)

One of these lists, price examples, and explanations, can be found at:

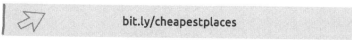

bit.ly/cheapestplaces

Per country overview

The Highest Cost of Living

1	2	3	4	5
Switzerland	Norway	Venezuela	Iceland	Denmark
126.03	118.59	111.51	102.14	100.6

6	7	8	9	10
Australia	New Zealand	Singapore	Kuwait	UK
99.32	93.71	93.61	92.97	92.19

11	12	13	14	15
Ireland	Luxembourg	Finland	France	Belgium
92.09	91.78	89.68	88.37	87.22

The Lowest Cost of Living

1	2	3	4	5
India	Nepal	Pakistan	Tunisia	Algeria
26.27	28.85	30.71	34.06	34.10

6	7	8	9	10
Moldova	Egypt	Macedonia	Syria	Colombia
34.72	37.22	37.41	38.24	38.92

11	12	13	14	15
Bangladesh	Indonesia	Georgia	Morocco	Philippines
39.22	39.35	39.56	39.78	40.00

This analysis took into account the cost of food at supermarkets, transport, restaurants, and utilities. Other essentials, such as housing, clothing and education were not included in the graphic originally posted on expat website MoveHub.

bit.ly/list-cheapest-countries

Instead of going for the cheapest accommodation, you could also check what amount of luxury a certain budget could afford you in various places. What can $1500 a month in rent get you in cities all over the world?

 bit.ly/1500-rent

Your cost of living depends on your lifestyle, of course.
Nomadlist.com has a very handy overview of different locations and the estimated cost of living for locals, expats, and nomads.
But there are many more factors. Mish and Rob share their ideas and calculations on their blog 'Making It Anywhere':

 bit.ly/digital-nomad-costs

You can find a lot of inspiration on the internet. This list with 12 unbelievably cheap paradises on earth, for example:

 bit.ly/cheap-paradises

Cost of living can even vary greatly within a country; cities, islands, and beachside resorts, are generally more expensive than small villages or rural living. Big cities, such as capitals, are usually most expensive.

Want to save on living expenses?
* Move to a cheaper (part of the) country.
* Living in a touristy area is more expensive than just outside of that area. Rural living is cheaper than city life.
* Eat and use local and seasonal produce. Imported/foreign products are usually more expensive.
* Why would you rent an office for your business? You can find flex workspaces and cafes with Wi-Fi all over the world. You can often rent an apartment with Wi-Fi in a metropolis for less than the price of an office.

JUST AN IDEA OF HOW LOVELY, LUXURIOUS & CHEAP LIFE CAN BE

* €0.90: cup of delicious espresso in a local village pub in Spain and Portugal
* €8: three-course lunch, including water, wine and coffee on a weekday in most restaurants in Spain and Portugal
* €19: a personal trainer (1 hour) in Curacao
* €22.50: two hour wonderful manicure and pedicure, at home or on the beach in Curacao, with French manicure or 'flowers' painted on your nails.
* €55: sumptuous dinner for four at the trendy Asian/fusion restaurant-chain, PF Changs (www.pfchangs.com) in the USA.
* €200: "Five days on a private island in Panama, with three local fishermen who caught and cooked for me and took me to the best hidden dive spots." (Timothy Ferriss, 2009)
* €125 "Rent a plane in Argentina, with pilot, driver and guide, to fly over Mendoza. Beautiful views over the vineyards and snow-capped peaks of the Andes." (Timothy Ferriss, 2009)
* €150 per month: a full time housekeeper in Indonesia. (bit.ly/cheapcountries)
* €180 per month: a private driver in Jakarta, Indonesia to drive you around up to eight hours a day. (bit.ly/cheapcountries)
* €300 per month: a modern, simple apartment in Bali, Indonesia. Beautiful, luxury, private villas are available at (for us) incredibly low prices.
* $750 per month for two people: average cost of a Finnish couple who have been traveling 4.5 years all over the world. This includes lodging, transportation, clothing, and laptops that they needed for their work (writing books).
* €800 per month: luxury living on Koh Samui, Thailand, including scooter rental, eating in restaurants, etc. (André, 2013)
* $15,000: A VIP wedding with 80 guests in a 500-year-old museum in Bogota, Colombia. Including the location, masses of fresh flowers as decorations, and a luxurious dinner, drinks, party, and top service for all guests.
* Under €20,000: Buy an ancient farmhouse in Romania or Bulgaria with several acres of land with fruit trees.

5) BARTERING AND SHARING

As the ideas of nomadism and minimalism are becoming more popular, the general attitude towards the concept of ownership is also changing. More and more people are sharing their houses (short term rent, Airbnb.com, nightswapping.com etc.), selling and swapping used clothes (Vinted.com), and renting cars peer-to-peer (Turo.com). Companies that enable sharing and peer-to-peer deals are growing in popularity. For digital nomads, these alternatives to ownership have many advantages:

★ Convenience - you have access to anything without having to own it.

★ Less stuff to keep, store, and maintain.

★ Reduced fixed costs.

★ By buying less, we are reducing the planet's collective carbon footprint.

★ These sites are a great way to get in touch with like-minded individuals all over the world.

Be creative and find ways in which you can barter your skills for lodging, food, or other things you need.

Diana and Steven have been traveling through Mexico in their antique Volkswagen van since 2011:

Money is not our main reason to work; we find it more important to do something we enjoy. That's why we started bartering. In exchange for food, a place to stay, or maintenance of our van, we build people a website or help them with online marketing. The past year in Mexico, we haven't had to pay for even one night's stay.
– DigitalNomadz.nl –

6) TRAVEL SMARTER AND CHEAPER

Travel expenses will most likely take a prominent cut out of your budget. You can keep costs down with these tips:

* Travel less; spend more time in one place.
* Be flexible in your travel dates, times, and destinations; keep an eye out for special deals.
* Travel slower; consider alternatives to air travel: Rome2rio.com shows all transport options; not just planes, but also busses, ferries, etc., including travel times and estimated cost.
* Be willing to research alternatives. When you do fly, use the tips on the next pages to get the best deals.

WHAT KIND OF TRAVELER ARE YOU?
How much effort do you want to put into traveling and finding the cheapest prices?

Comfort traveler: choose one preferred airline and book most flights through them. Sign up for their frequent flyer program and collect miles, bonuses and awards. Frequent travelers sometimes get upgrades and other benefits. This might not be the cheapest option, but it's the most comfortable one.

Cheap traveler: if money is your scarcest resource and you have plenty of time, this is the strategy for you. Check all options for each trip/flight, pick the cheapest one, even if that involves inconvenient travel itineraries, basic service, longer travel times, connections, layovers, etc. You'll collect miles, but they'll be spread over so many providers/airlines that you'll hardly ever get a bonus. But you will get to where you want to be at the lowest possible expense.

Personally, we prefer a combination of those two extreme strategies. We try to travel on two or three airlines, where possible, to collect miles and awards, but still check the best option (price/travel time) before each flight. No more night flights, unnecessary stopovers, or long travel times for us, 'older' nomads! ☺

---

17 tips for cheaper flights

If you search and book your plane tickets using these tips, you can get cheaper tickets, great deals, and collect frequent flyer and other bonus points.

1) Keep your searches top secret for consistent pricing
Have you ever searched for a flight and then, each time you checked it afterwards, found the flight price increased? Based on the cookies in your browser, flight prices do increase when a particular route is repeatedly searched. The site i strying to get you to book the flight quickly, before prices get even higher. To get around this, always search for flights incognito or via a VPN (Virtual Private Network), to find the lowest prices.

Incognito browsing ensures that no history or other private data, such as cache or cookies, are left behind at the end of your browsing session. In Google Chrome or Safari, incognito is enabled by hitting Command (on a Mac) or Control (on a PC), Shift, "N". If you are using an older version of OS X, open Safari, then click "Safari" in the menu bar, and select "Private Browsing". For Mozilla Firefox or Internet Explorer, hit Command (on a Mac) or Control (on a PC), Shift, "P". This will open a new browser window where your information is not tracked, thus no longer inflating prices as you search. Your cookies are reset each time you reopen an incognito window. So if you want to start with a clean slate for each flight search (so your previous searches aren't "remembered", potentially inflating costs), close all your incognito windows, open a new one, and then perform your flight search.

Browsing privately by using a VPN has two advantages. First, a VPN is a secure internet network where data cannot be intercepted. Second, it allows you to access country-specific content. This way, you can also take advantage of location-specific airfare deals some airlines have. Esther uses Hidemyass.com because she likes the logo of a donkey diguised with a hat, coat and sunglasses, but there are many other VPN's.

2) Compare across airlines and flight search engines

No single search engine is consistently perfect. Since there doesn't seem to be one that gets the cheapest flight 100% of the time, you may need to try a combination of search engines to ensure you're not missing any results. Once you find a cheap flight, remember to always check if booking directly with the airline is cheaper. Here are some places to get you started:

★ Skyscanner.nl — Our favorite website for finding cheap airfares. It searches a wide variety of airlines, including budget carriers that other sites miss. It also allows you to see airfares for an entire month, in one window, so you can pick the cheapest day to fly.
★ Cheaptickets.com — Local sites like cheaptickets.nl or cheaptickets.es often give different rates, so make sure to check various sites.
★ Google ITA Matrix — Efficient search engine with a grid view of the cheapest flight dates.
★ Vayama — For international flight deals from the US.
★ Dohop — Good starting point if you are based in Europe.
★ Momondo
★ Cheapoair (U.S., Canada, U.K.)
★ TripAdvisor
★ Azair (Europe & Middle East)
★ WhichBudget (includes budget airlines, which many search engines don't)
★ Webjet – Note: only use this site to search, and then book directly through the airline, as WebJet will add an additional booking surcharge.
★ Liligo
★ Skypicker.com

3) Find the cheapest destination to fly to

If you have no specific location in mind, just look for the cheapest destination. Google Flights and Skyscanner have an 'Explore' feature that allows you to put in your home airport and find the cheapest deals anywhere in the world. If you're up for an adventure and want to let fate decide where you go, this is a good way to travel on the cheap.

Whether you know exactly where you're going or you just want to find the cheapest possible country to fly into, try Kayak Explore. Enter your departure city, then select a month or season to fly. Approximate costs then appear over hundreds of destinations around the globe from your departure point, allowing you to see the most cost-effective place you can fly.

This tool can also be handy to find out how you can cover the most distance at the lowest cost, even if you have a set destination. For example, you want to go to Barcelona from Los Angeles, but flying straight there is pricey. Use Kayak to find a cheap European entry point and then consider budget airline options to make your final connection.

4) Be flexible with dates

Airfares vary depending on the day of the week, time of year, and holidays. It is generally cheaper to leave on a weekday instead of the weekend. Off-season is way cheaper than high season for a specific destination. Some flights are cheaper when booked way ahead; others have great last minute offers.

★ Skyscanner and Google Flights give you the option to display an overview of flights and airfares for an entire month. Search separately for your departure and return dates (one way flight, even if you want to fly return) to find the cheapest dates. You cannot book flights on Google Flights, but it does have a handy map view, so you can see where the airport is.

★ Flyr (getflyr.com) lets you predict and lock in your airfare before you buy.

★ The Hopper app (bit.ly/airfare-predictions) predicts price changes for your trip, and tells you the right time to book. Data-driven advice shows you the cheapest times to fly, and how to save more by switching travel dates or airports. Apple named Hopper the best travel app of 2015.

5) Fly into alternative airports

Instead of flying to an expensive airport, fly somewhere nearby that is cheaper to get to. For example, London Stansted instead of Heathrow; Long Beach, rather than LAX; Eindhoven or Rotterdam instead of Amsterdam; or Girona, rather than Barcelona. Sometimes traveling by bus to or from a different airport can save you money on flights. It may take more time than flying directly, but it's worthwhile if that means you're saving some serious bucks.

6) Try out budget airlines

Budget airlines offer significantly cheaper tickets than their full-service counterparts. Unfortunately, they are not always included in search engine results, so it pays to do an extra check.

When you're booking a budget flight, always read the fine print and know the budget airline's requirements & restrictions. The budget price comes with obvious compromises, such as less legroom, paid luggage, and no 'free' food/drink on-board (which by the way, is normally covered in your higher-priced ticket with full-service airlines). They might fly from a different airport. Some budget airlines also have ridiculous rules. Ryanair charges a hefty fee if you don't print your boarding pass or adhere to their luggage allowance. Check these seven tips from thriftynomads.com:

 bit.ly/facts-budget-airlines

Wikipedia has a list of budget airlines per country:

 bit.ly/list-wiki-airlines

Let's all add to this Wiki to make it even more complete.

Use Twitter, Facebook, or regularly check budget airline web pages, to stay up to date with specials before they sell out. Air Asia, Jetstar, Tiger Air, and Ryanair are especially known for having regular deals.

7) Search for local airlines

While search engines are great, they do not always include small airlines, especially in less popular routes and/or in remote regions. If you're flying somewhere obscure, Google search and ask around for a local airline. In South America, for example, LADE Air in Argentina (flown by military pilots) has crazy cheap flights to Patagonia, which is, of course, not listed in mass search engines online. When you do find small airlines, even if they are listed in a search engine results, it often pays to check the company site, which may reveal exclusive online offers not found in a regular search engine. For example, Hawk Air in Western Canada offers weekly deals on certain days. It pays to double check!

8) Check different routes and book flights separately

Consider booking multiple legs of a long-haul flight individually, to slash costs. Sometimes you can save hundreds just by making stops on a long-haul flight, instead of flying direct. For instance, flights to Bangkok are often cheaper than flights to Myanmar, so you can first catch a flight to Bangkok and fly with a budget airline, such as Air Asia, to Yangon. The cheapest way to fly between Europe and the US is via Iceland (on WOW Air) or Norway (on Norwegian Air), so consider catching a budget flight to Reykjavik/Oslo and flying to the US from there.

Be sure to spread out your flights and leave enough transit time between each flight. We like tight layovers, but if your flights are not on the same airline, sometimes your luggage will not get transferred automatically, or you will have to go through customs and check in again. Esther experienced this, firsthand, when her Ryanair flight from Mallorca to Barcelona got delayed, and she just barely made it to the gate of her Qatar airways flight to Doha, already accepting that she would fly without her luggage. Unfortunately, she was not on the passenger's list, so first had to go to the check-in desk on the other side of customs/immigration, thus missing her plane. She found out the hard way that you will not be compensated if you miss your connecting flight on another airline, when flights were booked separately.

9) Consider 'hidden city' Flights

Sometimes a flight that connects in a city you want to go to is cheaper than flying directly to it. Book the cheap flight that connects in your desired city and hop off there, not taking the onward flight. Make sure you travel with hand luggage only, as checked-in luggage is automatically labeled through to your final destination. Check if the plane actually allows you to disembark at your destination, otherwise you'll be wasting rather than saving money. You need to be prepared to take some risks, as not all airlines allow you to do this. Some might even put you on a blacklist: Spirit Airlines has been rumored to do that.

Skiplagged.com is a web search engine for hidden city tickets. It has been sued by United Airlines, but is up and running again.

It should go without saying; this is risky for many reasons. If the flight you're on happens to be the same one continuing to the final destination, you could possibly not be allowed to disembark the plane. If your plane ticket only has the final destination printed on it, you may also run into troubles. Use at your own risk!

10) Use alerts to keep track of prices

Flight prices can sometimes drop with time. Skyscanner has a price alert service that notifies you as soon as the price goes up or down. This approach is great if your travel dates, and maybe even destination, are flexible.

11) When you know when and where you want to go, don't wait to book

If you need to fly on a certain date, don't wait on seat sales – your savings are generally bigger the further ahead you book. Budget airlines typically offer low rates as a baseline price, and as these tickets sell, the remaining ones increase in cost – very typical in Europe and Australia. If you know when and where you're going, don't wait on an unknown sale. More often than not, your biggest savings come from booking far ahead when you can.

12) Consider using a travel agent

Travel agents have special undercut rates that are inaccessible to the public, although this doesn't always ensure they can provide the best price. It is wise to do your own research first, find the cheapest flight, and present that information to them to see if they can match or beat it. This would be especially beneficial for long-haul flights, where even slight savings can equate to a few hundred dollars. Also, for complicated multi-city flights and round-the-world-tickets, the experience of a travel agent might come in handy.

13) Check if it's cheaper to pay in foreign currencies

Calculate whether the rate is cheaper if paid in another currency. Budget airlines will often make you pay in the currency of the country you're departing from, but sometimes you can choose your preferred currency. When Esther was in Colombia, local tickets paid in pesos were remarkably cheaper than the same ticket, with the same airline, paid in US dollars.

Note: make sure you're using a credit card that is free of foreign-transaction fees (more info on page137), otherwise your attempts to save money doing this will be in vain.

14) Subscribe to deals, promos and error fare websites

To stay informed of the latest flight promotions, there are several websites that alert you when there are flight deals, or so called 'error fares'; airline pricing mistakes. There are special communities of people who consider it a game to spot airline errors, book those tickets, and travel almost for free. Note that some airlines don't honor error fares, but many do, so if you want to play this game, wait a while before you make any travel plans after you book such a ticket.

★ The Flight Deal — focus on flight promos from the US
★ Secretflying.com — allows you to find flight deals and error fares from any continent in the world.
★ Flynous.com - a Europe-centric site that keeps track of discount flights, error fares and vacation deals to destinations around the world.
★ Flyertalk.com has forums where members post error fares and other great deals they've found.

15) Sign up for airline mailing newsletters

Airline newsletters often feature exclusive offers. These range from upcoming flight sales to mileage giveaways. Airlines also announce new routes via their newsletters, and these usually involve very low introductory prices. For instance, Esther was able to get on JetBlue's first flight from Curaçao to New York for only $200 (return!), with free champagne, cupcakes, and giveaways.

16) **Join frequent flyer programs and collect miles**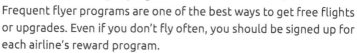

Frequent flyer programs are one of the best ways to get free flights or upgrades. Even if you don't fly often, you should be signed up for each airline's reward program.

There are three main airlines alliances you can join: 1) One World, 2) Star Alliance, and 3) Sky Team. An alliance is a partnership among numerous airlines. When you join the frequent flyer program of a certain airline, you'll be able to earn miles; not just for that airline, but also its partner airlines. Each alliance has its own pros and cons, so you want to make sure you join the one that's the best fit for your travel style and home base.

Sources: bit.ly/find-cheapest-flight
bit.ly/book-cheapest-flight
bit.ly/book-cheap-air-tickets

As I'm based in Spain, I fly with Iberia and British Airways most often and so I earn most miles on One World Alliance.
If I fly Qatar Airways, I get miles too in my Iberia rewards account as they are partners. This way I get to earn miles wherever I fly. I've been able to redeem free flights from Los Angeles to Madrid, as well as from Madrid to Singapore.
– Jacob Laukaitis –

|7) Flight hacking

According to the Travel Hacking Cartel, Flight hacking is "the democ-ratization of free and low-cost travel." Most travel hacking tips are only applicable to US citizens with access to credit cards; they can earn miles for almost anything without even flying; from spending money on a credit card, to joining a mileage dining program, to get-ting a hair loss consultation or car insurance quote, to taking out a mortgage. Sign up for credit cards that give away lots of miles upon registration, shop at airline partner stores such as Amazon, or par-ticipate in airline contests and giveaways. By having a travel credit card, you can easily pay for everything with the card and chock up to 36,000 miles a month, which you can redeem for a flight to Europe.

But the good news is: you don't have to be from the US to benefit from frequent flyer programs. If you can't collect enough miles your-self, you can easily buy them at BuyAirlineMiles.com. The rate is very favorable (approximately 2 cents per mile), meaning that, depend-ing on the season, you can fly to the other side of the world, busi-ness class, for $1,000 to $1,500!

More info and pro tips:
* The Travel Hacking Cartel guarantees you four free flights a year if you follow their instructions: bit.ly/cartel-travelhacking. Chris Guille-beau started this very professional 'movement'. There is a fee, but the first 14 days are only $1 and worth trying.
* Rolling Stone magazine wrote a story about "the man who trav-els the world for free": Ben Schlappig, a famous travel hacker: bit.ly/flying-for-free
* Ben's site onemileatatime.boardingarea.com offers an incred-ible amount of info and tips.
* millionmilesecrets.com
* www.flyertalk.com
* www.extrapackofpeanuts.com/start-here World travelers Travis and Heather share their travel hacking tips.

Daniela Ramos (1994) is a blogger and copywriter from Mexico. She has lived in the US and the UK and writes mainly in English. By camping, staying with friends, and hitchhiking, she manages to cut costs and visit many countries per year.

I do a bunch of things – web design, photography, fashion retouching… These are my favourite type of gigs as I am a visual person. I also write about travel sometimes. Even though it is not what I would like to do for the rest of my life, it has become my biggest source of income.

Since I was a kid I often changed locations due to my dad's job. I later moved to Florida with my mother. A year later I moved to New York City by myself and soon after I found myself residing in London. Then back to Mexico, where I began studying and working at a marketing company but that proved to be against what I had imagined my life would be (I shiver when I think back to those times, it was what I can only describe as life-sucking). This is when I knew a change was needed and I began establishing an online presence.

When I told my father my plans to leave university and travel, he simply replied saying "When you were eight years old, I realized this would be the life you would lead, that you were a free spirit and not meant to be trapped in school, and there is so much more you will learn out there than sitting on a desk". My mother did not believe me when I told her only the morning before my flight. She supports my decisions and is happy that I am living the life I chose even if sometimes I scare her to death.

One thing I discovered is that travelling with little to no money is possible. I often hitchhike and that removes any transportation costs I could have. I try to couchsurf whenever possible and I often sleep outdoors. The only times I spend money on hostels is when I have work to turn in. Cooking your own food is also a big money saver. I also try to spend a big chunk of time in a single place as opposed to moving around all the time (although sometimes I do that). This has proven to be more cost effective and good for my sanity and work.

I toured Ireland last month with my good friend Patrick. I know: Patrick. Isn't that the perfect name for Ireland? We got around hitchhiking, wild camping and sleeping in abandoned castles. I've also slept in the streets of Verona, Dublin, Budapest and in a myriad of gas stations around Europe. Hitchhiking through the Swiss Alps was also a highlight for me as I ended up in random villages that I would have never ever found on a travel guide. In Mexico I got invited to spend the night at a couple's house that was full of chickens running around everywhere. I could go on forever...

Relationships are probably the toughest aspect of full-time travel. I can't remember when was the last time I went out with someone without knowing there was a deadline. For this very reason I have become a bit cold-headed and always make an effort to not get too close (I know, it's not the best thing to do but after several heartaches you sort of transition into this). The same goes with the people you meet on the road and the friendships you make — there always comes a goodbye.

My top priorities for the next few months are Romania, Bulgaria, the Balkan coast, Iran, Jordan, Georgia and Turkey. Furthermore, it is my dream to head towards Southeast Asia (I know, as a digital nomad, it is quite unusual that I haven't been there yet). Another idea I have is to cross Russia and Mongolia into China by hitchhiking. Africa is also at the top of my list, but it shall wait a couple of years (but you never know, it was in my plans to be in Asia by now and for some reason I am in Slovenia). I never plan anything anymore and just go with the flow.

 http://bit.ly/im-dani

DECLUTTER YOUR LIFE

Life is much easier if you don't have a lot of stuff. Anything you own, you have to either drag along, or store somewhere. You have to secure, insure, and protect it. You can lose it, get robbed of it; it can get damaged or break down. So 'stuff' not only costs you money, but also attention, and therefore, energy.

The new hot trend, even among sedentary people, is to 'declutter'. Get rid of as many things as possible that:

⭐ you hardly use

⭐ are easy to replace, buy, rent or borrow when you need them

I move to a new country every four months. Everything I own, fits comfortably on my back. So it takes no longer than ten minutes to pack up everything and be ready to go. Last minute trips have never been so easy! – **Colin** Wright – Exilelifestyle.com

Hardly anybody finds cleanups 'fun' to do. Try to avoid the common pitfalls with these tips from the pros:

⭐ Minimizing is a lifestyle, not a trick. It's not a cleanup so you can buy more stuff.

⭐ Ask yourself each time: do I really need this? Is it worth taking with me or putting it into storage?

⭐ By selling, giving away, or throwing out what you don't like or use, you only keep the things that you actually use and like.

⭐ It helps to think differently about your stuff: "I am not the owner of these things. I am their temporary guardian; I feel free to pass them on."

⭐ Japanese cleaning consultant, Marie Kondo, is very strict. She only keeps the things that 'spark joy'.

So go ahead now. Make a choice: keep, store, sell, give away, recycle or throw away.

Take your time

This process of de-cluttering takes some getting used to, and the actual letting go of things may be quite difficult in the beginning. Most people feel overwhelmed at first. Go step-by-step, room by room, box by box. Ask others to join you in the experience. You need some practice to really get into this. Our experience is that you go through various 'cycles'; you get better at it and have more fun with it the more you practice. Let go of the idea that you have to do everything at once. In the first stage, shift through 20% of your stuff, for example. Go through everything again a few weeks or months later, and you'll find that you can easily let go of another percentage.

During the first round of de-cluttering, I thought, 'I just can't give away this book or this shoe.' A few weeks later, I changed my mind and got rid of them. After four months, our whole house was empty.
– Diana –

Esther, for instance, had given away a lot of books, but wanted to save her more-than-fifty Lonely Planets for some sort of sentimental value. They used to look so nice on the bookshelf, remember?

A few weeks later, she decided to only keep the Lonely Planets of countries she still wanted to visit, and the ones that contained her notes of past trips. That meant half of the guides could be given away. A while later, she looked at the remaining guides and figured, "When I'm finally visiting those countries on my wish list, will I take along that old Lonely Planet? And if I haven't looked at the notes in some books in twenty years, will I ever be bothered to do so?

Most guesthouses and restaurants I highlighted don't even exist anymore!" And with that thought, she was finally able to let go of the last Lonely Planet guides. Others were happy to receive them, and Esther had gotten rid of yet another box in her storage.

THE QUICK WAY - BY MINIMALIST PATTY GOLSTEIJN

As a digital nomad you want to live as light as possible. You probably don't have years to take a small step every day. You want to declutter in a rigorous way. How?

"Get a suitcase. Or two. The maximum amount you want to travel with. Put them on your bed. Open them. Instead of getting rid of things, you now only get to choose what to take with you.

That can be quite a scary approach, but also refreshing. Suddenly a lot of things don't make sense to want to keep. A big blender will take up way too much space. And you can get another one in an instant. There's no emotional attachment. This goes for all your furniture and kitchen equipment. You only need some clothes, toiletries, important legal documents and items that contain memories that can't be captured in a photo.

You'll start to realize that 99% of the things around you are for practical use only. They are replaceable. Just knowing that will make it easier to get rid of everything that doesn't fit in your suitcase."

Patty knows what she is talking about. In 2013, she moved from Rotterdam to New York with only one suitcase and a carry-on backpack!

On her blog, Patty Golsteijn provides more practical tips and examples.

 pattygolsteijn.com

Inspiration

Ever heard of the global 'tiny house movement'? More and more people are giving up their 'normal' house to live in the smallest possible house, with as little stuff as possible. Do a Google image search for 'tiny house', or check:

bit.ly/tiny-house-movement

We were fascinated by these interviews with six people who have taken minimizing to the extreme. One of them, Andrew, only has fifteen material possessions!

bit.ly/own-nothing

MINIMIZE YOUR STUFF

Need some help to overcome the common barriers when trying to sort out the stuff you've collected so far?

Sentimental value

"Oh no, I can never let go of THIS! It reminds me of..." The greatest barrier to decluttering is things of sentimental value. That drawing your 2-year-old niece made for you. The t-shirt of your favorite soccer team. The bible your grandmother gave you (even though you are not religious). To preserve the memory, you can take a picture of it, then let go of the physical thing. If you are not sure yet, save 'the thing' in a box for a while. You will find that eventually you don't need the 'thing' anymore.

Collections

Cleaning up large collections, such as books, photographs, clothing, or all those little knick-knacks and loose papers, can give a real kick. Put little knick-knacks and frills in a box and see if you miss them. No? Then you can get rid of the entire box. Take pictures of your fondest knick-knacks if you want to keep a souvenir.

Do you keep a box with craft supplies? Shells, stones, or pieces of wood you have collected, pretty papers, paint, glue. How often do you use it? Maybe it's better to give it away to someone who actually uses those beautiful things. Or you could organize a craft party for friends.

How many (hotel) soaps and samples do you keep in your bathroom? Give them away.

As a child, Esther collected stamps. Perhaps there was a rare stamp in one of the books she kept all those years. Perhaps not... Is that a reason to keep the boxes, with mostly nonsense, for years? She put her entire collection on Facebook as a giveaway, and made some-body extremely happy.

Books

Shelves overflowing with books lend a wonderful atmosphere to your house, but moving heavy boxes full of books in and out of storage is not so nice. In storage, you will also lose access to your books. Ask yourself the same questions for every book, 'Am I going to read it again? Can I make someone happy with this book?' Via Facebook.com, eBay.com, Bookcrossing.com, second-hand shops or charities, your used books can get a second life. Esther drove around with a box of books in her car for a while. Everywhere she went, friends were allowed to choose a book. Everyone liked the surprise present, and Esther was able to get rid of her books. Also, you can download digital versions of your favorite books, so you can always carry them with you.

Photos

"I have been to the exact same place! Wait, let me show you the pic-tures." And then what? Are you going to get your photo album out of your backpack? Shoeboxes full of photographs, or even albums, take a lot of space, and they're hardly ever in the same location when you need them. Especially when you are travelling, putting your photo albums in storage is like never seeing them again. The solution is to digitize them and keep them on your laptop or in the cloud.

Esther likes to carry all her photos with her —always— for books or blogposts she is writing, presentations, her website and social media posts, journalist requests, and friends and family all over the world. So many times this came in handy for unexpected meetings or requests. She keeps all her photos in Apple's iPhoto application (soon to be replaced by Apple's 'Photo'). The original iPhoto library is not on her laptop, but in Dropbox.com, so she will not lose her photos in case her laptop breaks down or is stolen.

You can scan the negatives of analog pictures, individual photos, or even entire albums. Photomyne.com is a special app that recognizes and scans individual photos from your albums.
Even snapping pictures of your photos or albums with a good smartphone gives amazing results.

It is best to name, date, or tag your pictures right away, but don't let that stop you. You can tag and name all you like, later, since you'll always have the files with you. The important thing is to have everything accessible in digital format.

Clothing, shoes & accessories

"All my clothes fit in one suitcase!" Wouldn't that be a wonderful and very practical thing? Patty Golsteijn has a very handy trick to make sure you only keep the clothes that you actually use. "I hang all my clothes in my closet. Hanging is much better than stacking. After wearing and washing an item, I hang it in front on the closet. If I notice that the clothes in the back are not being used, I throw them out." Patty owns only one handbag. "So I never have to remember where my keys and wallet are."

Esther had been lugging an exclusive evening dress and matching shoes around for years. "It was a beautiful dress; it had been very expensive, and perhaps I would need it again one day. But then I haven't worn it for ten years. And if I ever go to a formal event again, who says that I want to wear this particular dress? I finally gave the dress to a second hand shop and never looked back."

She also collected a lot of beautiful necklaces and earrings through-out her travels. "But I actually always wear the same earrings, and the necklaces stay mostly unworn in a box. If I take them with me on a trip, they often become damaged and tangled. So I decided to give them to my friends."

Seasonal stuff

Snowboards, camping gear and Christmas decorations – we all keep things that are only used sporadically. Is it worthwhile to keep and store it, or would it be better to sell, give away, or recycle that stuff? You can always borrow or rent things when you need them.

Skis, snowboards and matching shoes, are often only used once a year, sometimes even less. If you're traveling to the ski area by plane, you must now pay extra to take them on board. If you are going ski-ing for only a few days, renting gear is even cheaper than bringing your own. It saves you from travelling with a heavy bag or suitcase, and on top of that, you are always guaranteed the latest equipment when you rent, while the technology of your own "new" skis can be quite outdated after three years. Sometimes, on the other hand, it is worth it to keep your own shoes, or permanently lend them to a friend, provided that you may use them once a year.

For camping gear, the idea is basically the same. Do you want to own a tent, air mattress, sleeping bag, stove etc., or would it be OK to occasionally borrow or rent them?

Do you need to own a car?

Having a car means you get a lot of freedom. You can go where you want, when you want, and you can take stuff, and even other peo-ple, with you. You could even sleep or live in your car if you needed to. Esther was very attached to the idea of the freedom that own-ing a car provided to her (even though she only used it a few weeks per year). Only when she finally sold her car did she feel what real freedom is. No more parking problems or expenses, no maintenance worries, obligations or fees, no insurance, taxes, obligatory government tests, etc.

Esther realized that you don't need a car – you need transport. And there are many other ways to fulfill that need:

* Public transport
* A bike (many cities have special city bike programs)
* Ride shares
* Hitchhiking
* Rollerblading, skateboarding etc.
* Walking, running
* Taxi, Uber.com or Easytaxi.com
* Renting a car (check the car rental insurance icarhire.com, which provides year round coverage all over the world for only €130 per year.)

Hire or borrow a car:

* SnappCar.com
* Lyft.com
* Blablacar.com
* Car2go.com

In 2011, Daimler introduced Car2Go.com, a white Smart car with the convenience of a smartphone. Everything is digital: the contract, locating a free car, opening the door and keeping track of the 'rental minutes'. You can leave the car in any parking and just walk away, because the bill is paid automatically. At this time, you can find Car2Go in about thirty cities, from New York to Chongqing in China. Amsterdam is the first city where all Car2Go smarts are electric cars.

DIGITIZE AND ARCHIVE

You rarely have all your important papers at hand when you need them. By scanning them, storing them in the cloud, and organizing them well, you will always have them at your fingertips, even when you are on the road. This applies to your personal administration, insurance and souvenirs, such as art work, love letters, and photographs, as well as for business documents, such as contracts, business cards, and notes.

Advantages:
- ★ Access anytime, anywhere, to anything
- ★ Smart search functions
- ★ Easier sharing and collaboration
- ★ No storage space needed for paper copies
- ★ Reduced risk of losing/damaging/quality of paper
- ★ You have a backup in the cloud

When Esther got into a car accident in Curacao, her travel insurance documents were stored somewhere in the Netherlands. "Luckily, I had already scanned all my important documents. Via Evernote.com, I could immediately access my insurance papers and get everything organized," she explains.

If we ask you to show us your business registration or high school diploma, how long would it take for you to get to it? It's probably in a box, drawer, or storage somewhere. Esther is an Evernote fan: "I type 'Chamber of Commerce', or the name of my high school in Evernote and all relevant documents show up in seconds."

Google 'Evernote + tips' to see what clever things others do with Evernote.

Do you keep loose notes, flyers, cards, and clippings with fun things to do when you're in Barcelona, interesting websites or books, or that lovely little hotel in Bali? Scan them into Evernote and voilà, you'll always have them at your fingertips, easy to find, and no more paper.

Does your bank still send paper bank statements to your mailing address? You probably put them in a folder or drawer, and never look at them again. But when you're traveling and want to check if your bankcard hasn't been skimmed or if some exotic airline hasn't charged too much, then you won't have access to your statements. Most banks now have an option to switch to electronic bank statements. Some (like ING) even have a very handy app that lets you access your account from anywhere. If there is no other option than paper statements, have somebody at home scan them for you, so you always have access.

HOW TO DIGITIZE
You can have your archives digitized by a specialized company or by a (virtual) assistant (see page 224 for more info on VAs). However, it is also very easy (though time-consuming) to do it yourself. We find the following apps and devices useful:

Before, we used the Fujitsu ScanSnap; a mini-scanner that can handle multiple pages/pictures in one go, up to 12 pages (double-sided) per minute. It uploads your scans directly into Evernote, if you want. (bit.ly/fuji-scansnap)

Then, we found the Turbo Scan app. With this app on your iPhone, you can easily scan documents, receipts, etc. The SureScan feature lets you take three pictures of an important page, which are then combined by the app into one highly legible page. The scans can be turned into a PDF, sent via email, or saved to your camera roll. (bit.ly/turbo-scan)

But then Evernote launched their app Scannable. The app automatically identifies the document to be scanned; you only have to point your camera, no need even to click. The quality of the scan is very good. Of course, this app lets you save in Evernote, but also in PDF, and can be shared via email, etc. (bit.ly/ever-scannable)

Modern smartphones take such high quality pictures; most of the time that's all you need. A quick snapshot of your passport, important papers, a phone number, an article, or other note, means you will always have it with you. Esther had all her photo albums digitized by a VA who just took pictures of each page of the albums. Good enough is good enough.

WHERE TO KEEP YOUR ARCHIVES

Some digital nomads like to keep all their files in one place. Personally, we prefer to store things in multiple locations. First of all, you run less risk should something go wrong with a particular server. Also, there are many apps and programs that are conveniently specialized in photos, searchable files, receipts, etc. Our favorites are:

Many people know and use Dropbox.com. You get 2GB of free storage, and you can buy or earn more, if other people sign up through your reference. Dropbox also allows you to share specific folders for easy collaboration with team members or, for example, your assistant. Esther took her Dropbox use to an extreme. She keeps all her files in Dropbox. That means all files on her laptop automatically synchronize with her Dropbox account as soon as she is connected to Wi-Fi. Even if she loses her laptop, she can access her files, photos, and documents, from any computer. You can get a Dropbox Team account of 1TB for $795 per year. If you share this with up to five team members, it amounts to $159 per person per year, and each of you gets 1TB! Even within a team, all files are separated by team member; you cannot get into each other's files, unless you specifically share them.

Google Drive (drive.google.com) offers 15GB of free storage, which you can use for email, documents, photos, and almost anything. You can work in one document with multiple people. The last version of this book was edited in a Google doc, with André working on it from the Canary Islands and Esther from Mallorca, Amsterdam and on a cruise ship to Brazil. You need to be connected to the internet to connect to your drive, and for changes to be saved.

Evernote.com. This program is an absolute must. You can save anything, from documents and photos, to notes and even web pages. Esther keeps all her important documents in Evernote. The program uses advanced text recognition, so you can even find things within documents you haven't named or tagged or didn't put in a specific folder. If you need the proof of ownership for your house, for example, you just search the words "purchase contract" or "notary", and the address of your house.

You could save your photos directly to Dropbox, but then you would miss some useful features (like editing, face recognition, creation of albums and events), which specialized software like iPhoto (apple.com/mac/iphoto), Picasa (picasa.google.com), Flickr.com, and Shoeboxapp.com have built in.

Apple's iCloud.com lets you store music, photos, and documents. iCloud automatically creates a backup of your last 1000 photos and syncs your music, ebooks, address book, and calendar on all your devices.
Apart from your laptop or phone, you can store your music on Spotify.com, iTunes (apple.com/itunes), Match (apple.com/itunes/itunes-match), or SoundCloud.com. Some features are free, for some you'll have to pay a small fee. In exchange, you get access to an almost infinite music collection.

Esther, a real Mac fan, explains how she set things up: "I use iCal for all my appointments and birthdays. It syncs both through iCloud and my Gmail address, so I have everything on my laptop, phone, and in the cloud. I chose to enable 'Time Zone Support' (in calendar> preferences> advanced), to show everything in European time, no matter where I am in the world (most of my appointments are in Europe). That way, I always know how to interpret my calendar. When you turn time zone support off, all appointments are shown in local time. This means your appointments 'jump' to a different time when you are traveling and I never know if it is correct or not."

She uses her Apple Address Book to store all her contacts. In the 'Note' section, she keeps her CRM data; where she met that person, what workshop they participated in, etc. That way she has all the data about all her contacts in one safe place (it syncs with iCloud and Gmail).

Of course, Google also has a calendar and address book functions. The important thing is to store things online and to use the synchronization feature, which also creates a backup.

SMART TIPS AND INSPIRATION

★ In some countries you have to show your ID card, visa or social security number all the time, even when buying a box of nails at the hardware store. Instead of reminding yourself to carry the original document with you all the time, take a picture or scan it to Evernote, so you'll always have access to it.

★ You can also store your friends and family details and keep their passport number or a copy of their ID. Esther stores everything in Evernote, so she never has to ask twice.

★ If you still have a mailing address, ask somebody to scan your mail and email it to you once a month. You'll have direct digital access; no more paper files, forwarding, letters getting lost, passed due dates, etc. There are also professional services that can take care of this if you don't want to burden your family or friends.

* A few weeks before a presentation, there's usually a briefing. Esther likes to take paper notes, but has known many stressful moments when she wasn't able to find the notebook or remember her clients' requests on the day of the presentation. To prevent losing the paper version, she now takes a picture and stores it in Evernote.

* Esther recently had her complete media archive of interviews and clippings digitized. An assistant scanned the stacks of magazines and newspapers and uploaded them to Scribd.com. She organized them in 'collections' on a particular theme. TV interviews and other videos were uploaded to YouTube.com, and radio interviews are now stored on Soundcloud.com. This way, Esther doesn't have to keep the original files. The huge digital files are stored on other servers, thus avoiding costs for data use. On her own website she either embeds media from the other sites or simply places a link. Everything is easy to find and access, while backups are made automatically.

YOUR HOUSE: HOLDING YOU BACK, OR YOUR TICKET TO FREEDOM?

Do you own or rent a house or an apartment? This means you have a place to stay, to store your stuff, and to host your friends. But it also means monthly recurring costs and expenses. Does this mean you cannot live, work, and play, all over the world? Judging by people around you, economic forecasts, or that little voice in your head, you would almost think so. But there are loads of possibilities, really!

Are you renting?

In some cases, you may sublet the house for a short stay (Airbnb, Wimdu or similar sites) or long term (expats). Check your contract and/or contact the owner to make sure this is allowed. Some countries offer the possibility of a 'residence stewardship', where you let somebody legally take care of your house for a limited number of months –and pay rent– in your absence. Some people sublet their rental without notifying the owner. In most cases this works well, but you do run a serious risk of losing your place when they find out. The alternative is to share your place with house/flat-mates, thus reducing the costs. Worst case, you can let go of it altogether, so you don't have the burden and expenses of a fixed place.

Do you own a house, apartment, campervan, boat or otherwise?
If you are emigrating or planning to stay away for a long time, you could sell your house and use the money to invest, travel and live. Alternatively, you could rent it out (short stay or long term). If you live in or near a big city, chances are real estate agents are actively looking for (furnished) houses for their clients. With a bit of luck, you could even live off the proceeds.

Verify if your bank (where you mortgaged your house) allows you to rent out your house. Most of the time, this is officially not allowed; if they find out, you could lose your mortgage. On the other hand, as long as the mortgage payments are made on time, there is hardly any reason for the bank to check. Decide for yourself if you want to take the risk.

If you want to keep a room for yourself to store your things or to stay in when you are in your home country, you may consider finding a housemate (or more) to cover the costs of the house.

How about sharing your place with three other digital nomads? Depending on the number of rooms, you could all stay there at the same time, or each choose three months of the year. That way, you all have access to a fully furnished place, office appliances, such as a printer, and maybe even a car. It also provides each of you with a mailing address and a place to store some personal stuff and clothes. Plus, yearly expenses are cut in four!

Did you know you can 'house swap' your place with another home-owner somewhere in the world? Google 'houseswapping' and 'home exchange', or go to nightswapping.com. And if you have a creative background, check Behomm.com (a community of designers swapping their homes). This means, you can live in any place in the world without any extra housing expenses!

Some people find it's impossible to sell their house (even at a lower price than they anticipated) or to rent it out while they are away. In that case invite a house sitter who covers (part of your) expenses. Or even leave the place empty. Don't let your house weigh you down and limit your freedom. The total of your expenses may still be lower while living/traveling in a low-cost country, compared to staying at home. And even if your mortgage is always on your mind, wouldn't that burden feel lighter when you feel the sand between your toes on a tropical beach? Don't let your house stop you.

You don't have a place of your own?
Then you don't have to arrange anything and can just GO!

TIPS FROM THE PRO'S
Rent your house and make money via Airbnb. There are many 'congierge' services, offering to help you with managing your listing, receiving guests, cleaning etc. Stefano Cortevalante gives tips on how to maximize rental income: bnb-promotions.com

When I first started traveling, I was carrying way too much luggage. I was struggling in the train and metro stations, on the street, with stairs, etc. I was losing time, and I was getting in bad mood. Then I noticed that it wasn't just because of the weight and amount of stuff. Actually, I had a big issue with attachments that I needed to resolve. Now I travel with a lovely 12 kg carry-on that I don't entirely fill. It has really helped me enjoy my trips more, and save on luggage fees.
– Alicia Lima, customer service agent –

ON THE ROAD

We have collected some useful tips for your life on the road.

PACKING LIST

Depending on where you are going (climate), how long you are staying, and the nature of your trip (business, hiking, sports etc.), it can be a challenge to pack light.

- ⭐ Bring less. In the end, you always use less than you think.
- ⭐ Find multi-purpose items.
- ⭐ You can buy many basics, like shampoo, toothpaste, t-shirts etc. anywhere, so why bring them along?
- ⭐ Do bring everything you need for your business.

Traveling entrepreneur Jacob Laukaitis posted a picture of everything he brings on his 9-10 month trip through Asia (more about Jacob on page 120).

Backpack or suitcase?

Are you planning on doing a lot of hiking or walking? Then a backpack might come in handy. If you are mostly staying in cities, you'll probably want to opt for a suitcase on wheels. Do bring a small daypack for your laptop, which can also be used for city trips or short hikes.

If you can't choose, Eagle Creek developed a perfect 'in between' solution. The EC Lync System™ is an ultra-lightweight rolling bag that converts to a backpack (or duffel) and then collapses and stows away into a small stuff bag. This tough bag is covered by their awesome, 'No Matter What™ Warranty'. Their 'Pack-it' system consists of multiple folders and stash bags to smartly organize your clothing and other items by folding, rolling and/or stashing them. That way you can fit more into one bag and it is easier to find each item. eaglecreek.com/eclync-system

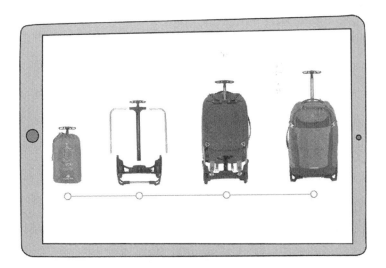

Clothes

There are many specialized travel clothes brands. These comfortable, light weight, non wrinkle, anti bacterial clothes can now also be worn casual or even for business. Some popular brands are:

> Ministryofsupply.com, Railriders.com,
> Oliversapparel.com, shop.bluffworks.com,
> bit.ly/mizzenandmain, bit.ly/exofficio-men

* Innovative designs, like this ultimate travel jacket, get a lot of support on Kickstarter (This one collected almost $8 million, while the goal was $20,000): bit.ly/best-travel-jacket.
* Joggjeans, both for men and women, combine the look of jeans with the comfort of track pants. Check out the new hybrid jeans: bit.ly/jogjeans
* Underwear, swimwear, and yoga/sportswear can often be multipurpose.
* Yoga/track pants can be worn on cold days, for casual wear, or even for horseback riding.
* Instead of bringing clothes for warm and cold climates, it's better to layer clothes. A windbreaker jacket combined with one or two (long sleeved) shirts, and a sweater or fleece, is often warm enough for moderate winters, so you don't need to bring a bulky winter jacket on a trip through various climate zones.

Shoes

Esther only brings two pairs of shoes wherever she goes:

* Flip-flops or sandals. "Ladies, these 'Crocs that don't look like Crocs' are my favorite sandals to wear in the shower, to the beach, and even to dinners and meetings. They look like leather sandals and are so comfortable, I even wear them for hour-long city walks." Meet the Croc huarache flip flops (bit.ly/crocs-flip).

- A pair of nice looking leisure/sports shoes to wear for hikes, casual meetings, and colder climates.
- Depending on your taste, and the nature of your trip, you might want to add real hiking shoes or dress shoes.

NO LUGGAGE?
Israeli designer Danit Peleg developed a fashion collection, which can be entirely 3D printed: bit.ly/3d-clothes

Is this the future of fashion; not bringing any clothes, but printing them in your hotel room?

Miscellaneous
- A yoga mat is multifunctional. Apart from exercising, you can use it as a picnic mat at a park, for sunbathing on the beach, you can sleep on it at airports and on trains, or use it as a sleeping mat for guests.
- Esther likes to bring a small (pocket) knife. It can be used to slice fruit or cheese, is handy for small repairs and might provide a sense of security on nightly walks. Don't bring it in your hand luggage or you'll lose it at the airport!
- A large shawl or pareo can keep you warm on chilly days; you can wear it as a skirt or dress, use it on the beach, or as a towel, or a sheet to sleep under.

Work
If you are going to work on the road, you have to bring everything you might need. Make sure to pack all tech gadgets in your carry-on luggage, because electronics are often stolen out of checked-in suitcases.

Your laptop
Let's take a closer look at the most essential item you need to be successful online; your laptop. Looking at (photos of) digital nomads

in co-working spaces, cafes and airports, and you'll notice that one particular brand heavily outnumbers all others: Apple. Digital nomads seem to prefer the MacBook Air or the newer generation MacBook Pro –they are fast, error-free, sturdy and lightweight– and yes, they look good, too.

Of course Apple's competitors haven't stood still either; there is a clear trend in laptops getting slimmer and more lightweight, whether they run Windows or even Chrome OS.

André bought his MacBook Air on the island of Koh Samui in Thailand. "It worked out about €200 cheaper than if I had bought it in Europe. The only 'downside' is that my keyboard has Thai characters on the keys too!"

Esther buys a new MacBook Pro in the US every year. "I would sell my 'old' one in the Netherlands, offering somebody a hardly used laptop at a very good price. Because of the exchange rate, I could get a new laptop 30-40% cheaper than in Europe; that way, I could get the newest model each year almost for free. Unfortunately, the exchange rate is now not so favorable anymore, though buying in the US is still about 10% cheaper than in Europe."

These are some of our favorite travel buddies:

✸ Many devices use the same cables and chargers, so eliminate and combine as many cords and connectors as possible. We love the colorful mini Incase cables. Why would you use long cables when you can connect any device with these tiny, happy ones? Bring a small US and European USB plug so you can charge your phone and tablet anywhere, anytime. We also bring both the European and US plugs for our MacBook charger. You can easily pop them on and off, and they hardly take any room. You could also use a multi-plug, but they are usually bulkier and contain a lot of plugs you never use. The headphones that come with your phone are suitable for listening to music, phone calls, whereas the tiny built-in microphone comes in handy for recording better sound in your videos if you don't have a real microphone at hand. (Photo 1)

★ (Noise cancelling) headphones not only block sound (very useful in an airplane), but are also a strong visual deterrent. They hint at people around to not bother you. These work wonders when you need some quiet time in a coworking space. (Photo 2)

★ Don't forget your internet banking digipass or other device. All cables, USB sticks, and other small electronics are stored in this small bag. The wooden iPad stand is great to be able to Skype, or watch movies hands-free, on your smartphone or tablet. (Photo 3)

★ Just in case you encounter a location with no Wi-Fi, but only cabled internet, or when Esther has to give a presentation with a beamer, she brings these two apple connector pieces. (Photo 4)

★ If you are planning to use local SIM cards, or going to a place where it's safer not to be seen with a smartphone, bring an old phone (plus charger).

★ Portable loudspeakers allow you to listen to your favorite music in your Airbnb place, on the beach, in a train, etc.

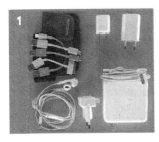
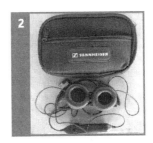

Jacob Laukaitis (1984) is an online entrepreneur, avid traveler, SEO specialist, and an occasional tech writer. Originally from Lithuania, he learns something new in every country, and is looking for business opportunities everywhere.

"I've been living this nomadic lifestyle for about two years now. During that time, I've traveled to 25 countries. I've motorbiked through islands in Thailand and the Philippines, hiked an active volcano in Indonesia, learned how to surf, gotten my deep-sea diver's license in the Gili Islands, explored new cultures and met dozens of wonderful people.

All through this time, my only possessions have fit into a small backpack. (Incidentally, it's the same backpack that I used to carry to school back in the day). I've found that owning things is simply impractical: You need to take care of it; it attaches you to a specific location; and it's usually more expensive than renting. I also haven't had a fixed address in the past two years because I rarely spend more than a month in a single country. This means that I'm free to go anywhere I want whenever I want. I can hop from Thailand to Japan to Indonesia without spending months selling my things and renting out my apartment. I simply buy a flight ticket and leave.

"After every one of my adventures I give a lot of thought to what I've seen, learned and taken away. In Japan I learned the value of selflessness and of caring deeply about the wellbeing of those around me. In Myanmar I learned that happiness is in no way defined by the money you have. In Vietnam I understood the importance of family. These experiences certainly go a long way in shaping the way I approach my life, but they're also becoming the basis of my professional thinking. They help me see opportunities outside the west, and create products for underserved societies.

"I launched my first company at the age of 15 and have been running my own ventures ever since. I went from establishing an online bookstore to popular content websites in Eastern Europe, amassing millions of unique visitors and tens of millions of page-views to ChameleonJohn with multiple projects in between. ChameleonJohn is an online coupons company, which has helped tens of thousands of people save on their online purchases in the United States. We established the company in May of 2014 and have grown to a team of 20 people full-time. We actually encourage employees to spend time away from the office. We're confused when somebody asks if they can go to their friend's graduation party or their mother's birthday. As long as they're delivering results, they are free to do whatever they like. We are also giving away $15,000 every year to students in need with our scholarship program and have donated money to hundreds of non-profit organizations.

Digital nomadism has the potential to make the world a little smaller, and digital innovation a little more inclusive."

 www.jacoblaukaitis.com

WHERE TO STAY WHILE YOU ARE TRAVELING

Usually you do not need a home, but rather a roof over your head and a bed. There are many ways to accomplish that, from free-accommodation to low-budget, from luxury to cultural exchange. Alternative 'living' can be much cheaper, more fun, and more adventurous than you might think.

In many countries you can rent a reasonable room for €25 per night. That amounts to approximately €750 per month. How does that compare to your current rent or housing costs? In addition, you do not have to furnish the place, clean it, pay for utilities, internet, or maintenance. An arrangement like this is very flexible; unlike a 'fixed' home base, these expenses stop when you don't use the place or when you travel on.

Below, we list various housing options, from free to luxury. Personally, we now prefer private rooms to dorms, and usually even stay in an Airbnb rental or hotel rather than a hostel, because of the level of comfort, privacy and the kind (and age) of people staying there.

Do not ask me

where I am going,

As I travel in this limitless world,

Where every step I take

is my home.

Dogen

House sitting and pet sitting

Did you know that you could become an official 'house sitter'? This can be done via a website or agency, but you can also use your own (social) network to offer your services. You make sure someone's house is lived in and protected from any intruders, during their holiday or absence. You take care of plants and/or pets and collect mail. That's usually about it. In return, you get a roof over your head, the luxury of everything the house has to offer, and sometimes even a small daily allowance. This can range anywhere from a few days to even months, in your own country, but also in distant, exotic locations; from simple apartments to unprecedented luxury estates. Well known house sitting agencies are:

 trustedhousesitters.com, housecarers.com
mindmyhouse.com, luxuryhousesitting.com
aussiehousesitters.com.au, housesitter.com

Some of them also offer pet sitting services. Google 'house sitting' in your own language for agencies specialized in your home country, or the local language of a place where you would love to house sit.

Home Exchange

Do you own a house? For many people, this is something that binds them to their home country. However, it can also be your 'passport' to other wonderful places (as explained on page 111). How about exchanging your home with somebody in a metropolis, like Hong Kong, New York or Berlin? Or maybe you prefer a tropical island? Home exchange means that you will live in another person's house for an agreed time and that other person will stay in your place. That creates a bond of trust; usually home exchangers take better care of each other's houses than random renters. Your housing involves no extra costs; you only have to pay your travel expenses. You will find several home exchange organizations on Google.

Nightswapping

If you have a place, you could also swap it against free nights anywhere. Other than home exchange, where you make an exchange deal with one other person and have to travel/swap at the same time, Nightswapping.com offers more flexibility. When people stay at your place (whether you are there or not), you earn points that you can spend within the network; anytime and any place you choose.

Couchsurfing

With seven million locations, Couchsurfing .org is the biggest 'chain' in the world offering free places to stay with likable hosts all over the world. Through Facebook, you can get acquainted in advance. Hosts offer a sofa, a place to lay your mattress, and sometimes a real guest room. Couchsurfing also lists events for hosts and their guests. A great way to meet new people.

Cultural exchange through Servas

Interested in cultural exchanges? Become a member of Servas.org. Their purpose is "to help build world peace, goodwill and understanding, by providing opportunities for personal contacts among people of different cultures, backgrounds, and nationalities." You will get access to host lists for the country of your liking, so you can contact hosts who share your interests. The idea is that you stay with a local host for two days. This is not just a bed, but a cultural (and sometimes culinary) exchange.

Work on an organic farm

If you are happy with a room and board, are willing to work and learn, and above all, integrate with the locals, then you might like WWOOFfing. WWOOF.net stands for World Wide Opportunities On Organic Farms. This was originally farm work, but it has become so diverse that hosts are now sometimes based in a city.

Friends and family tour

Visit your friends and family all over the world, and you can usually stay with them for a while. Planning a tour, mapping everybody you know, can be fun and rewarding in many ways. If you don't have friends all over the world yet, it's easy to find new friends through Facebook, forums, and other social media sites. Be creative! Ramon Stoppelberg (24 years old at the time) traveled the world completely free for two years through his website letmestayforaday.com.

Cheap accommodation

If you are traveling low budget, Hostelbookers.com is the obvious booking engine for dorm beds or cheap private rooms. Sites like Hostelworld.com and Lonelyplanet.com also list affordable accommodations. The cheapest option is usually a dorm room, where you share a dormitory with several others. If you prefer the privacy of your own room but don't mind sharing a bathroom, this option is usually low-priced, too.

Airbnb and other private rental sites

Find the best, cheapest, and/or most special accommodations, from private providers. Whether you're looking for a cheap room, a private villa with all the trimmings, or a good location to give a workshop, it is an ideal alternative to expensive and impersonal hotels. You often end up in special places in local neighborhoods rather than in tourist locations. Apart from Airbnb.com, there are similar sites, like wimdu.com, vrbo.com en roomorama.com.

Founded in 2007 by two guys who were frustrated about the lack of available hotel beds during the South by Southwest conference in Austin. The guys finally rented a spare room with an air mattress in it, hence the name Airbnb.

As a side note, Airbnb is a favorite with bloggers, thanks to their affiliate program. If new guests sign up through their invite link, both inviter and invitee get a $25 credit. If a new host signs up through the invite, both get a $75 commission.

So, if you don't have an account yet, claim your bonus of $25 via one of our affiliate links:

 bit.ly/airbnb-andre or **bit.ly/esther-jacobs-airbnb**

Hotels

If you prefer to go the traditional route and want to book a hotel room, Hotelscombined.com does a good job of comparing the big hotel aggregators. Booking.com and Agoda.com usually offer huge discounts. Some hotel chains offer regular promo's, which usually are good deals, such as 'pointbreaks' and 2-for-1 nights by IHG group.

Bring your own home

For a relatively small fee, you can buy a mobile home, campervan or boat you can use to live and travel simultaneously. Many people adopt this way of life temporarily; for example an overland trip from Central America to southern South America. However, it can also be a more permanent lifestyle. More and more people choose to live the mobile life. Some go even a step further and build their own 'tiny house'; a mobile mini-version of a house. Google 'tiny house' to learn more and see inspiring photos of this 'movement'.

Special deals

Look for special offers, like relocation cruises. Cruise companies sometimes move their ships from one part of the world to the other when seasons change. Since these trips are one way, and offer fewer stops than a 'normal' cruise, the prices are extremely low. For example, Pullmantur.es moves their ships from the Mediterranean to the Caribbean each fall. You can book a nine day cruise from the Canary Islands (Spain) to Brazil for €230. You get food, board, entertainment and travel, for a price that normally would not even get you a cabin! In spring, they offer the same deal in the opposite direction. More information about this cruise in PLAY page 273.

INSURANCE

There was a very cautious man
Who never laughed or played
He never risked, he never tried,
He never sang or prayed.
And when he one day passed away,
His insurance was denied,
For since he never really lived,
They claimed he never really died.

Few things in our society are so fear based as insurance. Ads and commercials constantly remind us of dangers and possible harm. They pretend we will only be safe and feel comfortable when we buy their insurance; legal, home, medical, dental, accident, travel, liability, funeral insurance, pet cover; you name it, they make it sound like you really need it.

Life is full of risks. How do you deal with this? Are you creating a feeling of 'false security' by trying to cover everything? Even the most comprehensive coverage does not mean you'll never have an accident, get sick or die. Some people want maximum insurance, just to 'play it safe'. Others don't take any insurance at all and "will deal with it when the occasion rises". The best strategy is to insure only the bare essentials and keep a small buffer for unexpected issues.

Imagine the worst thing that could happen. If you have enough savings to cover an emergency like this, then you do not need additional insurance. Instead of paying premiums to an insurance company, you just create your own buffer for emergencies.

How annoying it may be, most of us would financially survive a stolen laptop. The biggest risk (apart from being sued and court cases) lies probably in healthcare and particularly a serious accident or sickness. If you're not wealthy enough to cover a major disease treatment, hospitalization abroad or repatriation to pay out of pocket, then take out insurance with the highest possible deductible. For a relatively low fee you'll be covered for emergencies and you can live the rest of the time as if you have no insurance.

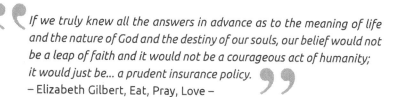

If we truly knew all the answers in advance as to the meaning of life and the nature of God and the destiny of our souls, our belief would not be a leap of faith and it would not be a courageous act of humanity; it would just be... a prudent insurance policy.
– Elizabeth Gilbert, Eat, Pray, Love –

EXPENSIVE EMERGENCIES

One of the leading travel insurance companies gave us concrete (scary!) examples of the worst that could happen and the price tag attached.

1) Malaria in Burkina Faso

Woman (49), severe form of malaria. Local care of low level. Ambulance flight was arranged. Kenya was not secure, therefore to South Africa. Total cost: €105,000

2) Bus accident in Brazil

Man (35), brain damage, fractured vertebra, broken knee. Repatriation to The Netherlands. Total cost: €77,000

3) Spider bite in Australia

Woman (29), treatment and evacuation €11,000

4) Complications of pregnancy in Indonesia

Woman (32), premature birth. Ambulance flight; treatment in Singapore. Total cost: €45,000

5) Terrorist attack Indonesia

Man (33), medical evacuation to Singapore because required assistance could not be given locally. Total costs, in particular due to stay in Singapore, +/- $300,000

- His cover for emergency and evacuation was max $100,000
- Part was excluded because of 'act of terrorism'

Please note that one day in a hospital in the US will easily set you back $10,000.

Most countries have obligatory health insurance for their residents. In some countries, like the UK, medical services are free. But when you travel you need an additional travel insurance to cover extra expenses abroad and repatriation.

Having only travel insurance won't help. These are meant to compliment your existing health insurance. Note that most travel insurance pose a limit to the number of days per year that you can spend abroad and/or travel consecutively. Also they are meant for holidays only, not business travel. So when prompted the purpose of your trip when you are claiming expenses, make sure not to state 'business'.

When you move to another country you can get health insurance locally or get an ex-pat insurance from your country or origin. If you are going to travel or backpack for a year, maximum two years, you can find suitable insurance, provided you will return to your 'home' country after your travels.

Digital nomads often don't have an official residence and therefore have trouble finding a suitable (health) insurance. Not being registered as a resident in your home country often excludes you from subsidized health insurance or free medical services. Not being an expat or backpacker severely limits your possibilities. Some travel insurances allow you to travel for up to two years. Check extremely well what is and isn't covered and under what conditions.

Health insurance companies offering international coverage are: Allianz, BUPA, Nordic, NOW Health intl, William Russell Elite FMU, ALC Health, Cigna Advance and Interglobal Ultracare. Prices vary between €110 and €250 per month. All of them exclude the USA, except for emergencies. Allianz is often used by digital nomads. Again, carefully check the terms and conditions, to avoid being denied help and/or reimbursement once you make a claim.

When joining a new insurance, they will ask for pre-existing conditions. You are legally obliged to give them information about illnesses or operations you have had. If any of your future claims involves anything remotely related to such condition, most insurance companies will not cover this. One of the advantages of the obligatory health insurance in your home country is that insurance companies do not have the right to refuse to insure anybody or to include pre-existing conditions. So if you have a 'medical history': hang on to your 'home' insurance!

Esther got kicked out of the health insurance she had been with for 43 years, just because her city de-registered her from her home address. She could not get insured as an expat (no new country/address) and was uninsured for several months. Only when she was visiting an IKEA on Mallorca island (Spain), she stumbled upon an IKEA Family poster announcing that IKEA was offering health insurance. For roughly €45 per month you can visit all the medical services in the MAPFRE network. She chose the second option: for about €65 per month she can choose her own doctor, hospital etc. all over the world and get 80-90% reimbursed. You do not need to be a resident of Spain to qualify for this insurance; all you need is a NIE number. This 'social security number for foreigners' can be obtained by spending a day lining up at the NIE office and filling in a Spanish address on the form (might be a friends address, could be an Airbnb address). The NIE form is valid for three months, but they usually don't stamp a date on the form, thus validating it indefinitely... This IKEA Family offer (underwritten by MAPFRE) is only valid on the Spanish islands (Baleares and Canary Islands), not on the mainland.

TELECOMMUNICATIONS

Of course you want to stay in touch while traveling. First, consider your basic strategy (or your own combination of strategies), and then look into practical solutions:

* Minimalist
* Local
* Comfortable

Minimalist

This strategy focuses on keeping your expenses to an absolute minimum. Use Wi-Fi where possible for email, internet, calls and messages (Skype, Facetime, Whatsapp, Viber, VoiP, etc.). Most hotels, apartments, and private houses have internet access nowadays, as do cafés, restaurants, shopping malls, public and co-working spaces. So with a little planning, you can be online as much as you like. You don't even need a SIM card or a phone plan. If you want, you can request a Skype phone number to give to your contacts, where they can reach you when you are online, or leave a message when you are not. It might be a good idea to manage expectations and add a line to your profile/email signature to explain that you are not always online, but will respond as soon as possible when you are.

Local

If you always buy a local prepaid SIM card and credit, you can make local calls wherever you are, even if you are not in a Wi-Fi area. The big advantage is that locals can reach you on a familiar number; many people are still somewhat put off by an international number. Another advantage is that you can always receive calls, whether you are in a Wi-Fi area or not. Check the specifics of your provider to see if you have to pay for incoming international calls. Receiving text messages, even international ones, is mostly free. Often data allowances can be bought prepaid as well. If your international contacts don't like to change your phone number for each country you travel to, you could get a Skype number, which will forward to your local phone number. That way you are the only person who needs to make the effort of keeping track of each new local number. In addition, you can use Wi-Fi where possible, like the minimalist.

Comfortable

If keeping your own phone number, always being available, and/or data access, are important to you, then an international plan might be the solution for you. They're not as economical as the strategies mentioned earlier, but they are (should be) hassle free.

The following international providers are worth considering:

* Vodafone RED Business: A great phone plan for business users, Vodafone offers one rate for unlimited calls, and high data use in 43 countries; mainly Europe, but also Australia. Details vary per country. The German Vodafone RED limits the number of weeks you can spend abroad; the Dutch plan does not have such a limit, so check your local offer. Esther had a Dutch plan and could call for free within the Netherlands, within those 43 countries, from those countries to the Netherlands, and to the other 42 countries. However, calling from the Netherlands to other countries was not included. Vodafone charged high rates for this. So it might be worth strategically choosing the country you want to base your plan in. Chamber of commerce registration required. Google 'vodafone RED Business' for the information page of your country.

* World SIM card (worldsim.com). Some in-flight magazines feature ads for this SIM card that works all over the world. 'Business nomads' Abel and Adrienne (page 49) are very excited about World SIM. You get a number that can be reached anywhere in the world, and the call and roaming charges are very reasonable.

* Truphone.com offers worldwide coverage on one plan, up to eight international phone numbers on one SIM, and local rates for calls, text and data, in 66 countries. Sounds like every digital nomad's dream, doesn't it? Esther used Truphone for a year and was very happy with her integrated Dutch, Spanish, and USA phone number, as locals always got to see a familiar num-

ber. However, in Colombia she could not call or receive calls for a week. Customer service was very friendly, but not effective at all, and invoices were a mess, even with the feedback she gave regularly. A Dutch friend in New York had the same negative experience. Decide for yourself if you want to try. Truphone only serves the business market, so you need to have a company registration.

★ Make sure you know what is included in your plan, and regularly check your bills. Roaming (international calls or data) is often ridiculously expensive.

★ Bring an extra phone for an extra SIM card (some phones carry twoSIM cards), so you have access to two numbers at the same time (for example, your 'home' phone number and your current local one).

★ Save a picture of the 'credit card' you get with your SIM: it states your PUK code, which you have to enter in case you use the wrong PIN code three times.

★ Write down the IMEI number of your smart phone, in case it gets stolen, or better: save it in Evernote or 1Password.

★ Turn on 'find my iPhone' so you can locate the last place your phone was seen, and block it completely in case it gets stolen.

Internet

No Wi-Fi available? Create your own network! By taking advantage of widespread mobile phone networks, you can turn 3G/4G coverage into a Wi-Fi signal.

★ MIFI: Many providers now sell small MIFI boxes (about €100, -) for use with a local 3G / 4G pay-as-you-go data SIM card. Buy a local SIM card in each country to avoid high costs. The device provides Wi-Fi for up to ten devices (laptops, smartphones, tablets and printers). It is battery powered, so you can carry it in your pocket. You can also get a 'dongle' for your laptop, but these can only run on one device at a time.

★ Personal Hotspot: Within the countries included in your phone plan, you can use the personal hotspot function in your smart-phone to create a personal network you can access with your lap-top or iPad. It uses your 3G or 4G, so make sure your data use is included in your plan to avoid high roaming costs. It is easy to set up: go to 'settings' on your iPhone, turn 'personal hotspot' on. You get a code to link your laptop or tablet, which you only have to enter the first time you use your personal hotspot.

★ Lantern: this is a device that gives access to the 'Outernet', wher-ever internet is censored, expensive or not available at all. This means access to weather maps when you're sailing the ocean, political information in countries that censor their internet, and access to Wikipedia for remote schools in Africa. Lantern is still in development, but promises to play an important role in remote and difficult areas of the world.

Check their crowd funding page for more info:

bit.ly/get-lantern

Texting, calling, and videoconferencing
Skype.com

You probably know that you can use Skype to make free (video) calls. You can have meetings, conduct coaching sessions, and keep in touch with friends and family. But there are many more possibilities:

* Call several people at once; like videoconferencing.
* Send almost free text messages to mobile phones. (Sender is your Skype name, so make sure to put your name in the text to make sure the receiver knows it's you.)
* With Skype credit, you can call all over the world at extremely low rates, also (mobile) phones of people who are not on Skype.
* Skype calls can be forwarded to your cell phone when you are not on Skype. This means you can be reached through Skype, even when you're offline. This is especially useful if you have a new local number in each country. Instead of sending that number to all your contacts, you can tell them that you can be reached via Skype and that all calls will be automatically forwarded to your new local number. You can even apply for a special Skype phone number, so you only need to give out one number. Callers won't even know that they are calling you via Skype.

The quality of Skype calls varies, depending on your internet connection, the number of users, etc. Sometimes it's crystal clear; other times it's not so good.

Facetime (apple.com/mac/facetime)
Free video calls to other Facetime (Apple =) users. As long as you are in a Wi-Fi zone, or use your data plan, you can call and receive calls. This feature is built into your iPhone, iPad and MacBook. If you look up a contact in your address book, you will find the Facetime option below their details. Click on it and the person will be called automatically.

Whatsapp.com, Viber.com and *Facebook.com*

Whatsapp and Viber were already popular for sending text messages and pictures. Both now also offers calls. Facebook already offered PMs (Private Messages), but now also enables free calls to other Facebook users. All calls and messages are free as long as you are in a Wi-Fi-zone.

Web.whatsapp.com is very easy to install on your laptop and integrates seamlessly with your phone WhatsApp.

Google Hangouts (google.com/hangouts)

You need a Google/Gmail account to use this great video conferencing service. On André's Mac it did not work with Safari or Firefox; only with the Google Chrome browser.

FINANCIAL TIPS

When you're abroad, the most convenient way of getting the local currency is to withdraw money from an ATM, using your bank card (not credit card!). Some ATM's (in supermarkets, at airports etc.) may charge an extra fee; this should be indicated on the screen. Debit cards or credit cards can also be used for withdrawals, but much higher fees are charged. We usually keep these for emergencies only. Be aware that exchange rates can differ greatly between one bank and the other. On top of that, they may add commission when you withdraw in another currency, as well as a fee for doing so outside your home country.

The only way to avoid ATM/card fees is by exchanging your home currency for the local currency, either before setting off, or by 'importing' your currency and changing it locally. Check both exchange rate and commission charged to find the best deal. In some destinations, banks will charge outrageous exchange rates and fees, meaning you'll be better off exchanging your money on the black market. Always ask locals for instructions.

Bankcards and credit cards can be blocked, damaged, stolen or lost. Be sure to always have a backup card or alternative with you, since it can be a hassle to get a new one sent out to you, especially when your physical location keeps changing.

> *ATMs in Spain return your card before dispensing the money you're withdrawing. In many countries, it's the other way around – money first. Guess what happened to me in Thailand: I took the money and completely forgot about my card. To make things worse, this occurred at an ATM I couldn't locate after I discovered my error.*
> *My bank insisted in sending the new debit card to my (old) address in Spain. – The rental contract of this apartment had ended before I traveled to Thailand.– Only after finding a long-term rental in Thailand could I change my bank account address and get my new card.*
> – André Gussekloo –

* Try to keep your bank account, even if you deregister from your home country. Opening a bank account without an address can be very difficult. Foreign bank accounts for non-residents might require lots of paperwork and charge higher fees.

* Make sure to provide your bank with a valid address where bank statements, contracts, and debit or credit cards can be sent. This can be a friend's or relative's address in your home country.

* Verify that your debit or credit card has been activated for use abroad. This often has to be done in the country of issue. You may want to raise the credit limit to provide for emergencies or serious shopping. These things are easier to arrange when done from your home country.

* If you don't have a credit card, this is the moment to get one. A credit card is safer to carry than cash, and is protected against fraud. It will be sent to the address on record, so do this before you set off on your travels. You may also be required to activate it by calling a Premium Rate phone number or making a first payment in your home country.

* Most countries now require you to use a PIN with your credit card instead of your signature. Make sure to store all your PINs safely, for example, in 1Password (see page 227).

* A digital nomad needs a PayPal account – both for sending and receiving payments. If you receive more than $3,000 per year on your account, PayPal will want to verify your address details. A scan of a recent bank statement or phone bill will suffice.

* For online banking, your bank will either give you a password and a list of TAN codes, or an electronic security token. If this security token is battery-powered and doesn't have a USB connection, it would be advisable to bring a spare security token on your (long) trip.

* Does your bank have a smartphone app? Install it so that you can check your balance, and make bank transfers anytime, without the need to open your laptop. We love ING's app.

* Your bank may not accept foreign phone numbers. If you don't know which number to give to your bank, this may be the right moment to get a Skype Out number, which is a virtual phone

number in your home country that redirects to your Skype account, or the local phone number at your destination.

★ Cards can be lost, damaged, blocked due to 'suspicious activity', or they can simply not be accepted where you travel. Ideally, you would have credit cards for different networks such as American Express, MasterCard, and VISA. The UnionPay network is gaining ground in Asia.

★ You can lose a big chunk of money when doing international transfers. TransferWise.com is a great alternative. It charges a flat fee and doesn't bend exchange rates to its advantage.

★ The app XE currency is useful to instantly convert the currencies you use most often to dollars, euros or your own currency.

★ Get your IBAN, Swift and BIC codes and save them in Evernote.

VISA

Depending on your country of citizenship / passport, some countries require a visa to let you enter. Usually you get a tourist or visitor visa, which limits your stay to 30, 60, or 90 days.

Carefully check the visa conditions for the country you intend to visit. Some visa can be obtained at the airport on arrival, while others have to be requested in advance at an embassy. Many countries (especially within the EU) have mutual agreements, meaning that residents of specific countries don't need a visa and can move freely between those countries. Nomadlist.com provides an advanced search option that shows the countries you can visit without needing a visa for your specific country of residence.

The system of visa issuance has focused mainly on leisure and business travelers. If you want to extend your visa, but can't prove that you are either on vacation, a business trip, or accompanying your expat partner, you might get into trouble. Global nomads should find their way in this system and sometimes even be willing to seek informal solutions. Often this means that you must leave the country for a while to return afterwards with a new visa.

Some countries (e.g. the US and Curaçao) require a return ticket to prevent visitors from lingering unintentionally. If you need proof of an onward flight, Flyonward.com can provide you with those details. If you booked a one-way ticket, you can 'rent' the details of the required return ticket trough them.

I first thought my Guatemalan passport would really limit my travels. However, without visas I can get to Europe, Turkey, Russia, Japan – in total to more than 65 countries around the world. It is a pain when I need visa to a certain country and I only can get it back on my country of origin. I've skipped those countries now.
– Alicia Lima, virtual customer support agent –

Working on a tourist visa
You are not allowed to work on a tourist visa; some countries have very strict policies. If only there were a visa that acknowledged and invited digital nomads, we wouldn't have to feel so anxious about working on tourist visas. Digital nomads are not typical tourists, but neither are they a typical business traveler. After all, digital nomads don't do business in the country they visit, or compete for jobs from the locals. Rather than working IN a country, they work FROM a country. Of course, there are areas with open borders, such as the EU for EU citizens, but the general rule is that you need a visa to enter or work in a country different from your own. So what visa should we get?

Most digital nomads get a tourist visa and motivate eventual visa extensions by their fascination for the destination – which is probably true.

If push came to shove, you could defend your choice for a tourist visa to immigration officials who question your activities. After all, you work for foreign clients while spending your income locally.
If this does turn out to be a problem, it will be complicated for authorities to prove that you were actually working. You could have been reading up on blogs you follow, or sending an email to your

family or friends back home. Online, there is a fine line between business and pleasure.

While laws and their interpretations will vary per country, it was interesting to follow the events of the 30th of September 2014, in Thailand. Immigration and police officers raided PunSpace, a popular coworking space in Chiang Mai (more about coworking spaces on page 237) and detained the digital nomads they found there. It turned out, the officers thought that PunSpace had hired western staff without work permits. When the owners made it clear that the farang were not being paid, but rather paid PunSpace to use their facilities to make their money overseas, the detained were free to go. So in the end Thai authorities seemed to be okay with digital nomads doing their thing on tourist visas.

However, they emphasized that you always have to have your passport with you or can be fined otherwise.

Read a first-hand account on bit.ly/chiang-mai-raid.

DEALING WITH BUREAUCRATS

"Give them what they want. Don't fight them on their terms."

For some people, each interaction with 'the system' is difficult. Garry Davis, the first World Citizen, expresses his dilemma: "Every time you must show your papers, you hand over a sliver of your freedom. The documents in fact legitimize the existence and superiority of the authority that has created them." Garry offers the following solution: "Data, facts and figures, are the talisman of the bureaucrat. So give yourself a number, date and address, help the bureaucrat to fill in the empty fields on the form. Speak his/her language. That way you begin the process of neutralizing (or charming) the bureaucracy/bureaucrat."

Garry shares ten tips on 'how to deal with bureaucrats'. Even though they date from the 1950s, when Gary traveled the world with his homemade world passport (page 43 for more info) and his typewriter, and drove many a bureaucrat crazy, most of them still apply to the modern digital nomad.

Get organized, stay organized

Know what you're talking about. Continue to ask questions; the bureaucrat you are facing probably only knows everything about his or her task, but doesn't know the big picture, as you do. If he can't answer the question "which authority decides this?" demand to speak to his supervisor. Always ask for the names and positions of those with whom you are dealing and make accurate notes.

Stay cool

You're right, and they are not. Stay calm. Make sure you get the truth without antagonizing the person you are dealing with. "Turn every command into a question."

Go to the top

Bureaucrats do not see us as people. They just want us to fill in the form, so they can send it through to the level above them. So if you have problems at the bottom of an organization, you also can go a level higher.

Assume you are right

By quietly informing people that they infringe on your (basic) rights, you make them feel like they are complicit in a possible crime.

Keep them informed

When you go a step higher, it is important that you keep everybody informed, including the 'lower ranks'. Once you publish your situation and treatment, things often suddenly start moving; not only within the organization, but also possibly elsewhere.

Keep track of the paper

In the land of the bureaucrats, it is important to have your files in order. No one else can collect as much information about your own 'case' as you can. Even if you, at some point, have to call in help from a lawyer, the media, or if someone higher up wants to help, they should know exactly what happened and when. Send all attachments in CCs.

Find the right words

It's not just about being polite; also use the right vocabulary, the correct terms/titles, and find the right tone. Speak the language of the bureaucrat. Refer to as many rules, laws and facts, as you possibly can.

Make yourself look good

It is important that you look neat and tidy. And ensure that your correspondence does, too. If your correspondence suggests that you do not care, then they will not either. If you look unkempt and jittery at an airport, you are more likely to be checked and called in for questioning. Make sure you do not stand out in a negative way.

Set a deadline

A request to an official body or bureaucrat without a deadline is an invitation to ignore or forget. You're the 'victim' here. By adding a (reasonable but clear) deadline to your question/request/suggestion/problem, you emphasize that you demand a solution and that you won't be easy to get rid of.

Remain firm

Even if you prepare everything well and take all the right steps, it may take a long time before a solution is in sight. Time is in favor of the bureaucrat, so he/she will always try to eke out a procedure in the hope that the problem (or the person experiencing the problem), goes away or gives up. Show that you are not bluffing; if you threaten with certain steps and the deadline has expired without result, issue a final warning and then execute your threat. Think of it as a game. If you make a move, it's their turn.

 'My Country is the World' by Garry Davis
(bit.ly/about-garry-davis)

TRAVELING WITH KIDS (OR PETS)

Can you imagine a better gift than spending more quality time with your partner and/or kids? To experience adventures together, taste new flavors, meet interesting people, and discover new places? Traveling abroad is beneficial to children and adults in many ways.

A nomadic lifestyle is certainly not reserved for singles or couples without children. Digital nomads traveling with children say it's easy enough; but admit they are traveling in a different way than they did before they had kids. You stay longer in one place and sometimes you have to plan ahead more than you were used to. Your perspective also changes; the main attraction of a place can suddenly be that nice playground instead of that beautiful church, that famous restaurant, or that attractive boulevard.

A recent Atlantic article examined the link between greater creativity and travel. Columbia Business School professor Adam Galinsky explains: "Foreign experiences increase both cognitive flexibility and depth and integrativeness of thought, the ability to make deep connections between disparate forms." Travel is beneficial because "the key critical process is multicultural engagement, immersion, and adaptation."

It's not just a person's creativity that will get a boost from travel. Their sense of trust in others benefits as well. "We found that when people had experiences traveling to other countries it increased what's called generalized trust, or their general faith in humanity," Galinsky said. "When we engage in other cultures, we start to have experience with different people and recognize that most people treat you in similar ways. That produces an increase in trust."

There's more! The Atlantic article quoted Mary Helen Immordino-Yang, Associate Professor of Education and Psychology at the University of Southern California; on the benefits of traveling for a person's sense of self. "The ability to engage with people from different backgrounds than yourself, and the ability to get out of your own social comfort zone, is helping you to build a strong and acculturated sense of your own self." Immordino-Yang concludes: "our ability to differentiate our own beliefs and values ... is tied up in the richness of the cultural experiences that we have had."

Education and Homeschooling

"I would like to travel, but my kids need to go to school..." Education is often cited as the biggest barrier to long-term traveling with children. But it doesn't need to be. We'll address three components:

1) Education laws: If you have children who are school age, they have to receive an education.
2) Content: your kids need to learn certain things, like reading, writing, math, languages, history etc.
3) Social skills: going to school provides valuable experiences in interacting with other kids

1) Some countries (the Netherlands and Ireland) have a 'school obligation', whereas most other countries have an 'education obligation'.
   a) If you aren't registered anywhere, then which law do you have to abide to? If kids and parents aren't registered, the schooling law doesn't apply. The teaching law, however, remains valid for all children of school age.
   b) You can temporarily live in another country and enroll your children in a school there. You must, of course, take into account the education legislation in that country.
   c) If you figure your trip is more important, you can always just go and accept a possible fine from the authorities. Choose your wording carefully when explaining your trip. Emigrating to (for example) Australia will get more sympathy from the authorities, then plans to 'travel for a year'. If you come back after a year and say, 'It did not work out in Australia,' then you have a greater chance that your kid will be readmitted into school without any trouble.

2) You could homeschool your child en route. Traveling with children provides valuable experiences for both parents and kids. The children live, experience and explore different cultures and languages. They learn to be flexible and see things in perspective. They will realize that the world does not revolve around them. They learn languages, geography, history, biology, and other lessons in real life. A traveling mother explained, "When we visited the ancient ruins in Greece, an American teacher was surprised that our eight-year-old daughter knew more about the Greek Myths than he knew. The secret? We teach her while traveling."

3) Instead of daily interaction with the same kids at school, traveling kids meet others of all ages, nationalities, cultures and religions, social backgrounds and learn to interact with them. They might play soccer in the streets with a group of kids they can't even communicate with. Or teach English to new friends on a beach. Siblings will also get different relationships through travel.

Self-teaching has many advantages. You experience intense moments with your child. You are flexible in your schedule. Far fewer hours per day are spent on education, than if your child were going to school. It has a positive effect on your child. The Association for Homeschooling explains, 'Homeschooled children are equal or even ahead in their school progress and social-emotional development compared to children who attend school. They cite similar or higher scores and are often socially skilled and mature. In addition, they easily adapt to the transition to college and their learning motivation is maintained or even increased. However, you should be aware that as a parent you will be heavily involved in education, meaning you'll have less time for yourself and your work."

TRAVELING FAMILY

Meet the Kortman family: Paul, 35, his wife Becky, 37, and their four kids — Alia (9), Josiah (7), Mathias (5), and Zander (3), who traded in their house for life on the road. Since March 2014, they've been traveling around the world, moving every three months or so. Dad sustains their family (and three full-time employees) with a digital marketing business.

Paul and Becky enjoyed traveling internationally as a couple before they had a family. "When we were teaching in Kazakhstan, we met many *third culture kids*." (A third culture kid is a child who spends a fair amount of time living in a culture other than that of his or her parents.) The couple were inspired to give their kids the same opportunities they witnessed in children who experienced life in different countries, including the ability "to help them avoid the consumerism and American-centric worldview they would have growing up in the states."

The Kortman children's lifestyle should go a long way in helping them grow up as open-minded, confident, and creative individuals. "It's most beneficial to our kids through firsthand experiences," Paul said. "They'll be watching a video on YouTube and comment, 'Hey we were there!' or 'That's not what the Philippines really looks like.'" He explained that the family experiences life beyond videos and books. "Our kids know stuff because they were there."

While being away from friends isn't always easy, and the kids miss out on some extracurricular activities, like music, dance, and sports, the freedom and flexibility that the Kortmans enjoy make the trade-off worth it.

To ensure their educational needs are met, Becky teaches the kids, mixing principles of homeschooling, road schooling, and unschooling.

After their first six months of traveling, they realized there wasn't a formal online place for nomad families to gather and receive support, so Paul and Becky co-founded NomadTogether, which offers support through education, tools, and a community forum.

The Kortman story: bit.ly/no-home-family
The family's website, HomeAlongTheWay.com
and their site about family travel: nomadtogether.com

Summarizing, we would say: don't let your family be a hindrance to living your dream life; instead make them part of the adventure.

★ Give your kids their own camera and marvel at how they see the world.
★ Always have the following documents with you (for example, in Evernote): the birth certificate of your child, if applicable, your marriage papers and a statement of consent from both parents that the other one is allowed to travel with the child. If you are a one parent family, you also need proof for this.

Much has been written about traveling with children. Many authors have combined their experiences and tips in a blog or book. Here are some links to inspiring stories and books, tips, and links about family travel:

* The Kings, a family living out their dreams since 2010, currently traveling the globe with a 4 & 2 year old: **akingslife.com thefamilywithoutborders.com**
* Family travel tips from ytravelblog: **bit.ly/travel-as-family**
* List of Lonely Planet tips by authors with kids: **bit.ly/travel-with-children**
* Lonely Planet family travel tips: **bit.ly/lonely-planet-family-travel**
* Lonely Planet forum with tips and questions from other traveling parents: **bit.ly/forum-kids-to-go**
* Rough Guides 20 tips for traveling with children: **bit.ly/children-traveltips**
* Lifehacker: how can I make traveling with kids less of a nightmare: **bit.ly/tips-travel-with-children**

Traveling with pets

When André and his girlfriend considered living the nomadic life, they worried about what to do with the cat they had just adopted in Spain. They decided to take Lima with them, and to resort to 'slow travel'. "We wanted to keep our little 'family' together and that a long flight to Thailand was just something we had to get through. We found out that Russian airline Aeroflot allowed pets to travel on board, and that the price was only €50," recalls André.

"It was definitely worth the trouble. Lima loved the pigeons she saw from our Chiang Mai window, had some unforgettable cat fights on Koh Samui, saw a snake slither through the bushes, and had lots of fun catching geckos."

ANDRÉ'S TIPS FOR FLYING WITH A PET

★ Plan ahead. Visit your vet months before setting off to arrange vaccines and certificates.

★ Depending on their size and the airline policy, small pets can travel in the cabin, in a bag, between the seats. You are not allowed to take them out, but it does give you the opportunity to soothe and feed them. Larger animals will have to travel in the luggage hold of the plane.

★ Sedation is not recommended, due to the different air pressure and the effects it may have on the animal. Rather than sedating, familiarize your pet with its travel container.

★ Make the trip as short and sweet as possible. Take direct flights or spend a few nights at a layover destination.

★ Prepare all the paperwork before leaving. Some quarantine and immigration offices will have the required documents on their website. Print them and fill them in, so that the wait for the required stamps is as short as possible.

★ When arriving at the airport for your flight, first go to the airline's ticket desk, as you will probably need to pay a fee, and take your receipt to the check-in desk.

★ If you're flying with your pet in the cabin, you can take it out of its carrier once you're through security. Be ready for lots of attention from fellow passengers!

★ Even if your cat or dog is normally very quiet, make sure to keep them on a leash at all times in unfamiliar surroundings, especially airports. They might panic and run off in an instant.

★ Putting a blanket over the pet carrier will calm your four-legged friend down during the flight.

As for Lima, she safely returned with André from Thailand, and has now retired to the Canary Islands, where she spends her days lazing in the shade. "I'm not sure I would do it again. It has probably been more stressful for me than it was for Lima," smiles André.

RELATIONSHIPS

Can you maintain relationships as a digital nomad?

The answer is YES. The nature of the relationships you have while traveling will be different from what you are used to, though. You will see less of family and friends back home. But when you do get together, it will be more intense; quality time. You will meet many new people and make new friends, but you'll have to accept that either you or they will leave after a few weeks/months, or go in a different direction.

Intimate relationships will be more rewarding, but also more challenging. If you meet a potential partner who lives in a fixed location, you could visit this person often, or decide to 'settle down' with them. They might want to try traveling with you. If you fall in love with another digital nomad, you will have a lot in common. But two free creatures, used to follow their own path, getting together will also pose some challenges. You will have to follow your own inner guidance. This means, most likely you will have to make some concessions to both travel programs and ideas.

Check the digital nomad-dating site: dateanomad.net and the Facebook group Nomad Soulmates.

I rather date travelers. Constant movement doesn't mean lack of commitment. As a matter of fact, it means I truly understand what commitment is. I'm committed with my own dreams and I'm not going to choose to be with someone because I feel lonely. I strongly believe that we travelers take decisions knowing and appreciating the freedom we have.
– Alicia Lima, virtual customer support agent –

One relationship that you'll definitely develop is the relationship with yourself. You will get to know yourself better. You'll have to deal with hardships, loneliness and with seductions, such as parties, nice beaches, cocktails, etc. You'll have to motivate yourself; look for meaning instead of just fun. You will get to know your strengths and weaknesses and, therefore, become a stronger person.

Relationship drawbacks of the digital nomad lifestyle that have been mentioned in various blogs:
- Loneliness
- Forgetting the last time you had a long-lasting relationship.
- Your friends will keep asking when your gap year will be over.
- Your family back home will start picturing horror scenes when you don't reply to their emails quickly enough.
- When you meet your friends back home, you might realize that you can no longer relate to them and it is hard to maintain a conversation with many of them.
- You become somewhat unattached to people, and even places, because everything becomes temporary.

It's amazing how many interesting, open-minded people you meet on the road; and these connections are not superficial or casual at all. I feel that through traveling, the chances of meeting your 'tribe' are much bigger than if you stayed in one place.
– Vera Ruttkowski –

Many digital nomads emphasize that it's important to them to be part of a 'tribe', a community. That is why digital nomad meetups, and other meetups of like-minded people, are so important to them. On page 265, you'll find a list of groups and meetups.

SAFETY

Just like in your home country, there are smart and 'not-so-smart' things to do. There are neighborhoods where you'd better not walk alone at night. Always ask the locals. Here are some general safety tips:

Personal safety

* Hitchhiking by yourself? Take a picture of the license plate before you get into the car, and app it to a friend. Take a nice picture of you and your 'host' and post it to Facebook (ask permission first). "This nice guy Peter from Berlin is giving me a lift to Dusseldorf. Good people!"

* There have been some reports lately of Couchsurfing hosts harassing female travelers staying with them. Carefully check your host's profile and references left by other (female) travelers. If in doubt, look for another host.

* Don't flash your smartphone, laptop, or other gadgets in the streets, especially poor areas. Even if it's an old model, or it was very cheap; they still look fancy and worth having/stealing, to some.

* In some countries, taxis can be dangerous. Ask locals what company to use and how to verify. In Bogota, Colombia, for example, you get a code from the taxi dispatcher and the taxi driver has to show you this code; otherwise, you don't get in.

* If your intuition tells you something does not feel right, listen to it and get out of there.

* Ask locals what (not) to do and where (not) to go. Some countries, like South Africa, have special 'rituals' for safely using ATM machines or for locking yourself into your own house at night.

* Companionapp.io is a personal safety app that lets a friend virtually accompany you on your walk home.

* Beware of pickpockets in busy, touristy areas. Never carry all your money, cards etc. with you or keep them in one place. Store them in different, safe places but always keep a small amount of cash ready to hand over in case you get robbed.

Virtual/digital safety

* When you use Wi-Fi (especially for payments or confidential information), create a VPN (virtual private network), using a provider like HideMyAss.com. That way, nobody will get easy access to your personal details.
* Turn off 'automatically connect to Wi-Fi' to keep control over your connectivity.
* Protect your passwords, PIN codes, credit card info, etc. Don't write them down and don't put them in a file called 'passwords'. Better to use a safe app like 1password (see page 227 for more info)
* Make backups! Don't keep the external hard drive with your backups in the same bag as your phone/laptop...
* Keep copies/scans of your passport, credit card, driver's license and insurance papers in the cloud, as pictures on your phone and/or paper copies, so that you'll always have access to these important details.
* Beware of 'skimming' when using ATM's. Use only often-frequented ATM machines, preferably during daytime with lots of people are around.

Of course, you have to be careful and use your common sense, but whether you are going to be led by fears or trust is up to you. Most people are good and honest and trustworthy, all over the world. Let's make sure our experiences and interactions with them are positive ones.

Tal Gur (1975) created financial freedom in one year, after being in $34,000 of debt. He now helps others to achieve the same freedom. Originally from Israel, he lived, worked, and traveled in over 50 countries across six continents. His main focus is personal development.

In 1996, aged 21, I fell in love with Australia during a long motorcycle trip in this remote, vast and spectacular corner of the world. After the trip, I went back to Israel to study computer science. Websites were completely new to that era and I found them fascinating. I started buying Israeli domain names for big companies and brands, and sold them to those companies later, managing to make some money.

However, the memory of my epic trip to Australia never left me. In 2003, after several years working in the high tech world, I made a decision to pursue every big dream I have ever had. I left my home country to live and study for my Masters degree in Australia.

It was quite complicated to arrange my visa for Australia, so I published a few tips on a popular Israeli forum for others wanting to live and work there. I was so passionate about Australia that I soon included more and more info about the country. People liked my forum posts. I got good feedback and also a lot of questions: 'How did you do this?', 'How should I arrange that?' To make life easy for everybody, I decided I should put all my knowledge about Australia on a website. The website (in Hebrew) became a big success in Israel, with lots of media attention. Still, I was just trying to share my passion and help others. I did not even consider that I could be making money this way. Until, one day, the first advertiser contacted me. Many more travel agents and migration agencies followed. That was the first time in my life that I got paid without actually having to work for it. At one point, the website was generating more income than my 'real' work. Still, I did not get it.

I worked as an IT manager and I had a good life; my company needed me. And I needed them, because I still had a significant personal debt. One fateful day in 2008, my bank statement showed a total debt of AUD$33,598.62. My credit card limit had been reached and I hit a financial, all-time rock bottom. The prospect of not being able to pay the rent loomed like a dark storm cloud on the horizon. I decided to start focusing on wealth creation and financial independence. To make my commitment even stronger, I opened a blog and publicly announced my new financial freedom challenge.

But in 2009, my parents got into a serious car accident. I hurried to Israel to visit them. I wanted to stay, but I felt torn; the company really needed me, but so did my parents. I made a very hard decision: I quit my job. I needed to make a huge shift in my life. I shared the news with my friends to further intensify my pledge to create financial freedom.

My plan was plain and simple: I would build informative and useful websites that would generate automatic advertising income. At that time, my Australia website was generating about $400 a month in income. In Australia, you can't live on that, so I decided to go to Nepal, where the cost of living was much lower. So after six blissful years in Melbourne, I sold everything I had, packed a small backpack, and left on a one-way ticket to Nepal. I became an online entrepreneur, working as a freelancer; even my old job gave me some work.

I decided to duplicate the success of my Australia website, and started a site about New Zealand. Although I had traveled there, I did not have enough information for the website. So I asked others to share their knowledge about New Zealand. Everybody is always willing to share his or her passion, just like I had wanted to share my love for Australia. So the New Zealand website also became a success.

I had just completed an Ironman Triathlon in New Zealand, after quitting smoking, and was thinking to myself, 'What if I translate everything I learned in the fitness realm to the realm of financial freedom?' Step by step, I reduced my expenses and created passive income in various forms. Now, after seven years, I still live off my online and passive income. It's hard work, but it can be done!

Since pursuing my first Australian dream, I found myself constantly seeking new challenges, overextending myself in all aspects of life, ultimately resulting in very happy and fulfilling journeys:

- Surfed around the world in places such as Brazil, Costa Rica, Peru, and Sri Lanka
- Explored spirituality and tried a 10 days Vipassana meditation in India
- Learned how to become a Muay Thai Kickboxing fighter in Thailand
- Completed a 12,000 km journey around Australia, cutting through the outback
- Train-traveled across Europe, drove around Italy, and motor biked through the Swiss Alps
- Trekked Everest Base Camp in Nepal and some of the most famous trails in the Chilean and Argentine Patagonia

Financial freedom is great, but it's definitely not about the money. Passive income can enable things, but personal development is what makes life worthwhile. I have had great experiences, like being on an amazing island in Brazil, drinking cocktails on the beach, having fun, partying, enjoying my financial freedom. I partied for 60 nights in a row while living in Melbourne, Australia. I celebrated carnival in Rio and Salvador, Brazil, learned Spanish in Buenos Aires, and completed a 30-day salsa journey in Medellin, Colombia. But still I felt like something was missing: meaning. That's why I went to Bolivia, the poorest country in the world, and ended up building a new home for a family that had lost everything in a mudslide in Peru. I also helped to build a school for a poor village in Dominican Republic and volunteered in an international autism treatment center in the U.S. throughout the summer.

We have an incredible chance, here on this planet, to create beautiful things; a real opportunity to live life to its fullest. But we can only accomplish this if we push ourselves far beyond our comfort zones, face our greatest fears, and take the risks involved in pursuing that which we truly want. That's what really gets me excited, what motivates me to create, to coach, to share.

What I like best about this life is the freedom it gives. Freedom to choose. That means moving towards things that you love, instead of acting out of fear. Life on the road is not all rosy. Trust me, I've had my share of struggles. What I miss sometimes is the depth of relationships. Many people you meet leave again after a few months. I also miss investing in a community. Being part of a community, a tribe. Therefore I now actively seek out tribes and invest in that. For example, I am a member of DNX and Dynamite Circle. They organize meetups in various digital nomad hubs. Whenever I get to a new place, I look up people of the same mindset who are already there.

Ever since I remember, I was intrigued by the endless possibilities of self-expression. I simply see life as a playground to express our deepest desires and experiment with the perceived limits of the physical world. I have come to realize that my life is not just one linear continuous journey, but more a recollection of different journeys and experiences. I've learnt that it is definitely not all about the destination, but more about the journey. And the greater the challenge, the more satisfying it is.

 www.oneyeartofreedom.com

TRAVEL BLUES

A lot has been said about the perks of digital nomad life. So much, that some have been accused of selling a dream. Let's be honest, the pictures of happy nomads on the beach with their laptops are not very realistic; you don't want sand and salt getting into your keyboard, and the sun makes it hard to see your screen. Even though the view is nice, it is really much more convenient to work in an air-conditioned office or apartment.

While nomad life certainly isn't a nightmare, it's time to take a more realistic look at digital nomadism. Life on the road is great and does guarantee some unforgettable experiences, but there are some drawbacks that can make this lifestyle a challenge.

Let's first get the digital nomad 'problems' as most people imagine them out of the way:

* Having to apply sunscreen before going to work.
* Having difficulty to decide where to go next – Bali, Spain or Costa Rica?
* The curse of the traveler – always thinking that there must be something more beautiful. But in the end, the beaches are beautiful everywhere in the world; it is the people that make it unforgettable.
* Having to live in a serviced apartment and having no control over your own laundry, as they do it for you.
* Working while lying down makes your back hurt.
* Spending the whole day in the pool/at the beach because it's laundry day and you don't have a shirt to wear.
* Going for a swim when the electricity or Wi-Fi goes down; all you can do is relax.

There are far more serious travel issues: work complications, relationship dilemmas, personal challenges and other annoyances, challenges, and setbacks.

The following (crowd sourced) list can be a reality check for budding digital nomads. Rather than imagining a life of cocktails and push-button income, they see what working online while traveling is really about. As you will see, some problems are absolutely trivial, while others are tongue-in-cheek, or simply won't apply to you.

The list may also serve as inspiration for professional problem-solvers: start-ups, established companies, and – dare we say it– governments.

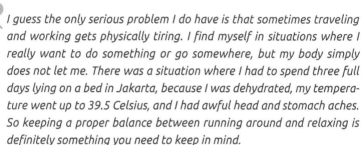

I guess the only serious problem I do have is that sometimes traveling and working gets physically tiring. I find myself in situations where I really want to do something or go somewhere, but my body simply does not let me. There was a situation where I had to spend three full days lying on a bed in Jakarta, because I was dehydrated, my temperature went up to 39.5 Celsius, and I had awful head and stomach aches. So keeping a proper balance between running around and relaxing is definitely something you need to keep in mind.

– Jacob Laukaitais –

Travel problems: Documents and Customs

* Having to guard your passport with your life.
* When you're filling out a form and they ask you for an address. It is completely unacceptable to state that you're without a fixed home base, apparently.
* When you are asked for proof of employment to get a visa.
* Having a passport photo that makes you look like a criminal and makes the immigration folks look at you like they can't decide whether to give you the stamp or put on the latex gloves.
* Getting asked for an onwards ticket to board a plane. Chances are you don't have one because the amount of freedom means never having a set plan.
* Visa rules that change constantly or are inconsistently applied. We bemoan the strictness of some countries' visa policies, but inconsistency (and the often expected bribes at some borders) can get really annoying and drain your time and energy.

Getting and staying there

* Time stuck in airports.
* The infamous 'chicken buses', combis, colectivos, you name it – Realizing that comfortable buses are a luxury for a very small percentage of the world's population.
* Having to find accommodation everywhere you go.
* When the apartment you booked looks completely different than the pictures shown on the website you booked through.
* Jet lag.
* Forgetting what seasons are.
* Staying healthy and fit can be challenging, as you have no time to undertake a sport. Plus, you are constantly trying all the foods from every country.
* Arranging gym access when you might be somewhere for a month or less is difficult. In a lot of places, they want to charge an arm and a leg for short-term access.
* Wanting to do the groceries, but finding out it is a national holiday.
* Trying helplessly to avoid every scam you've ever heard of (e.g. the tea scam in China).

★ Climates, seasons, and pollution. The cloud that hangs over Las Palmas (Gran Canaria) in July-August, the smoky season in Chiang Mai (February-May), Monsoon season in India, etc.

Tech problems

When technology fails, your work will take a beating. Are you prepared for the worst?

★ Your MacBook has crashed and now you have to travel to the capital to get it fixed.

★ Your charger is dead and you're in the middle of nowhere and that important deadline is tomorrow.

★ Having to decide which technology will be the most likely to actually work for an upcoming conference call or client meeting: Skype, Google Hangout, WebEx, Gotomeeting, Join.me, Teamviewer, Appear.in, etc.

★ CityMapper and Google Maps don't work well in many countries or cities. I've been lost in my apartment for three weeks.

★ You had your computer and electronics insured but once something happens you realize you didn't read that tiny text written at the bottom on white letters over a white background that mentions that it doesn't cover them if you dropped it (or whatever it is that happened).

★ Typing foreign language characters on a regular keyboard is hard. Typing English on that cheap foreign keyboard you got is also hard.

★ Not being able to work when it rains because it makes the Wi-Fi go down.

★ What? No 4G in this town?

★ Being stuck in cosmopolitan cities all the time, because remote areas don't do Wi-Fi.

★ Countries that make it hard to get a SIM card.

★ The everlasting search for stable connectivity.

★ Those expensive buses you take because they promise there is Wi-Fi on board; however, there is always a 'problem' with it and "they apologize for the inconvenience".

Cultural differences

* In some countries, finding out that 'now' doesn't exactly mean 'now now', and having a local appointment really can screw up your timetable.
* Being woken up at 5 AM by some random rooster.
* Forgetting that some things that are considered normal in your homeland aren't in others (for example, kissing strangers on the cheek).
* Occasional stomach cramps due to ever-changing foods and spices.
* Doctors and nurses' laughter when you show up in the Thai hospital after a scooter accident. Takes a while to find out they are not laughing at you; they are just nervous about having a foreigner, a wounded foreigner, in their hospital.
* Your Brazilian neighbors stay in the hotel to party (all night long, in their room, next to your room…), while you are there to be productive and work. Not a good combination.
* It happens to the best of us: customs officers searching your bag ask if you always bring sex toys on holiday. (For example, in Thailand, they are forbidden, but you can buy them on the markets.)

Time zones

* It's already beer o'clock in your previous time zone.
* Having to calculate time zones so your mom doesn't know you're awake at 3 AM when you answer her emails.
* Having to run from the bar for a Skype call to another time zone.
* Constantly having to remember the time in different parts of the world for your Skype calls with clients.

Money, banks, taxes

* High seasons and local holidays, because prices for everything go up.
* Always having to figure out how much "x" amount is in your currency to be able to tell if you're being ripped off. (The app XE Currency might help you with that: xe.com/apps)
* Changing currencies on a regular basis.
* Bank fees. ATM fees.
* Always having to be afraid of ATM eating your bankcard, or being skimmed or worse, robbed when you get money.
* Budgeting, and more importantly, sticking to your budget.
* Still having to file taxes for the country in which you have citizenship.

Your life –and business– inside a backpack or suitcase

* Having no dress shoes to wear when you need to attend a formal event.
* Suddenly realizing that your Facebook photos painfully point out your lack of a wardrobe.
* Not being sure what to pack. Your plan is to spend 90% of the time in the Caribbean, but what if you get the opportunity to fly to Greenland?
* Your gadget collection gets heavier and heavier.
* Having to carry every kind of adaptor there is.
* Constantly having to resist the urge to buy souvenirs or something nice you saw because you know that in the long run, it will only weigh you down.
* Missing having your own (working) space.

Homesickness

* The beer at home tastes better.
* Missing your country's cuisine.
* Missing your momma's comfort food.
* Missing out on important events back home, like weddings, funerals or the birth of your niece.
* My friends are organizing a party, but it's on another continent.
* Visiting the 'home country' feels like doing a tour, and the best way to visit your friends is to surf their couches.

Pressure

Traveling and working at the same time can really put a strain on you:

* You see exotic places, meet new people and have awesome adventures. But sometimes you just don't want all those new impressions and new faces. You don't want to live out of a suitcase anymore. You want to stay in one place, with people who know you and love you. Or maybe you just want to be alone for a while. Those moments will pass, but every traveler knows them. And if they don't pass, you can always hop on a plane to wherever feels like home to you.
* There is constant distraction, so you have to focus on what you want to do (work/play), where you want to go, etc.
* Lines are getting blurred (private/work), so you have to be your own 'boss'.
* Moving out of your comfort zone (every new destination is a 'reset'). Some nomads create their own comfort zone or familiar environment; they light candles or burn incense, waer headphones to play their favorite music or eliminate background noise. Little rituals that help you feel at home. You can recreate your work environment wherever you are, so you feel comfortable and not frustrated by whatever is going on around you. Everywhere is different.
* Constant change; even the simplest things, like doing your laundry, have to be 'reinvented' each time.

* Introspection: the act of self-reflection. Input, lots of thinking, impressions, people we meet, etc. It can be a lot to process. This can be both a challenge and inspiration.
* Loneliness, isolation, being one with the world, but isolated at the same time. You meet lots of great people, but everybody leaves at some point. Many nomads complain that relationships are shallower.
* Internet. This can be very annoying. Imagine you're in an Airbnb apartment and there's no internet. They said there would be, but there is not. Or worse, there's just enough internet so that it teases you, but you can't get any work done. A good tip is to have the host send you a screenshot of the speed test before booking. And even that's not always a guarantee. But remember that sometimes being offline can be more valuable than being online. Write, do creative work that doesn't require internet. Try to be comfortable with not having internet. Don't try to fight it. Embrace it.

Luxury problems
* Working at the beach sounds like a dream, but in reality, it is not so great. The sun makes it hard to discern what's on your screen, sand gets between your keys (and your eyes!), beach balls hit your head, the list goes on.
* On some occasions, we are labeled as 'bums', and we often have to explain that we aren't wasting our lives or ruining our careers by traveling.

Let's end on a high note
Despite all this, being invited to a trip the day before leaving and being able to say "yes" without even blinking; forgetting the use of excuses such as "I can't go, I have a job to get to"; not having to deal with that dreadful commute to the office every morning, and being able to choose when you want to work and when you want to be outside and enjoy your ever-changing surroundings is pretty darn great.

Vera Ruttkowski (1980) is a virtual assistant from Germany. She lived on Tenerife for two years, and is now exploring Asia for a taste of the digital nomad life.

After finishing school I started to work in an advertising agency and studied alongside this at a private university in the evening. I graduated in Marketing and Communications. I continued working in advertising agencies and then worked for several years in a software company as a sales and marketing assistant. After this, I switched again to work in an advertising and public relations agency. While I loved my work (at least most of the time) I always felt I had missed out on the chance to travel after finishing school and I hardly ever had any holidays. In the beginning I loved the lifestyle of working long hours, weekends and only socialising within the agency. The higher the workload the more important I felt - but after some years that started to change and I felt the need to do something different and to be free.

I grew more and more unhappy with my life, but I never really dared to make a change. Until life taught me the hard way, that sometimes there is no tomorrow. So I decided to have a 6 month break to get back to myself and find out what I would like to do and to change. A series of random decisions, serendipity and encounters brought me to Tenerife, one of the Canary Islands, to do an internship at a language school. I was the oldest intern ever, but I was happy.
I always loved the sunshine and the beach, so it was a dream come true to live on an island where you can go to the beach all year long.

When the 6-month internship ended I still didn't know what to do with my life - but I knew I didn't want to leave the island. So I started looking for a job, found one, and it lasted one month until I realised I couldn't get back into a regular 9-to-5 job where I had to fulfill tasks that didn't make any sense to me. So I tried to find something where I could use my experience and knowledge whilst being more independent, and found an offer for virtual assistants. First I started to work for an agency and now I work for my most of my clients directly. In the beginning I was teaching German to kids in addition to working as a virtual assistant so that I could have some form of a fixed income.

The pros of virtual assistant work are that –of course depending on the tasks that you have– you can follow your own time schedule. What I enjoy most is that I learn so much through this job and the different tasks I get. Most of the time my work doesn't feel like working at all because I'm doing things I really enjoy and find interesting.

A con is that, like all freelancers, you are exchanging your time against money. So, especially in the beginning you have to work much more than in a regular job to make a living. And as you depend on the jobs that your clients give you, the workload can vary very much from one week to another or even day to day. It can be challenging to organize yourself and the large number of tasks in hand, but this is a skill that I have perfected over the years.

Before coming to Tenerife I took a 3-month intensive Spanish course and tried to get from zero to fluent. Which of course didn't work. Especially when I had to realise that the Spanish in the Canary Islands is different. Also learning a new language in the country in which it is spoken, will bring you many funny situations when you try to communicate and just guess the words or use the wrong expression. Some words are just too similar to each other, like in Spanish cojines, cajones y cojones - but have a very different meaning. ☺

While I really love my new home here in Tenerife I feel it is time to move on, at least for a while. Due to my studies and jobs I have only travelled within Europe so far and I still want to see Southeast Asia. Thailand and Bali are good spots for digital nomads so I have chosen those as my first destinations. I plan to travel slow and stay at least 4-6 weeks in one place.

www.verava.de

*When work
is a pleasure,
life is a joy!*

Maxim Gorky

DO WHAT YOU LOVE

To make your mobile lifestyle sustainable and not just a temporary trip, you need to find a way to create an income. Don't know where to start? You're not the only one. We often meet people who have a strong desire to be a digital nomad, but who are at a loss on how to make ends meet in circumstances completely different from what they are used to. Whether they are overwhelmed by the possibilities, or think they don't have the skills required, the feeling of being stuck can be really frustrating.

And that is where this chapter comes in; we want to get your creative juices flowing. One way to do this is to give you lots of examples of what other nomads do for a living.

 If you think it's too difficult to work online, then you're probably overthinking it.
– Jon Yongfook, entrepreneur (yongfook.com) –

TYPICAL ONLINE JOBS
Below is a random list of activities that help digital nomads finance their travels. Which of the following strike a chord with you? The list is by no means exhaustive. Can you think of new jobs, for example, by combining a few of the activities below?

* Tax adviser
* Virtual assistant
* 'Infopreneur'
* Translator
* Online retailer
* Business coach
* Personal trainer
* Film maker
* Insurance agent
* Software consultant
* Author

- Drop Shipping
- Forex or stock trader
- Poker player
- Copywriter
- HR consultant
- Social media manager
- Travel blogger
- Video game tester
- Online teacher

Choose a job you love, and you will never have to work a day in your life.
– Confucius –

'MY JOB IS NOT SUITABLE FOR A DIGITAL NOMAD LIFESTYLE'

Some jobs seem like they were made for digital nomadism; they are performed entirely on a computer, and there is no requirement to work from a certain spot. Freelance web designers and copywriters are examples of such location-independent professionals; they can bring their laptop, board a plane, fly halfway around the world, and work from there. Their clients don't mind, if they even noticed it at all. However, the reality is that most jobs tie people to one place. A baker can't just jump on a plane and take his bakery with him. A medical doctor needs to see his patients. A police officer is bound to his station, and a road worker needs to work at a specific location, right? Does this mean people with these professions cannot become a digital nomad? The answer is: they can, but they will have to make significant changes to their work. If you have a job that is not suited to location-independence, there are three things you can do: work locally/offline, teach, or make a career change.

WORK LOCALLY/OFFLINE
You don't have to go digital. Sure, this guide is about –and for– digital nomads. Armed with a laptop, they can set up their office anywhere they can find an internet connection. But let's not forget that the laptop is just a means to an end; the end being freedom and the ability to travel.

Most types of work can also be done in another location or country. Working as a doctor in Africa, as a baker in India, or a security guard in Peru, might not make you a lot of money, but it offers valuable experiences. You could even sell bracelets on the local markets or fruit on the beach. If what you really desire is getting away from where you are currently, finding a similar job abroad could be a stepping stone to the digital nomad lifestyle.

TEACH WHAT YOU KNOW
You've worked with your hands for a long time. You have developed skills that others are dying to learn. One of the ways you can turn those into a location-independent business is by transferring your knowledge to others. Whether you do this through books and video courses, or more active channels, like coaching, mentoring or workshops; this can often be done from anywhere in the world. A doctor can even see his patients online. What if he specializes in digital nomad patients? They will appreciate his flexibility! The baker can offer e-courses in his specialty; the different ingredients, and exotic locations as a background, will only make them more interesting.
And if you do need to get together physically, why not organize courses or workshops wherever you happen to be? You'd be surprised at how many students will be interested in a tax-deductible trip!

MAKE A CAREER CHANGE
However logical becoming a teacher may be, it is a lot of work and requires a mix of skills and talent. If the idea of transferring your knowledge does not appeal to you, the other way to go location-independent is by making a career change, by deliberately choosing

a job or building a business that allows you to work from anywhere. In the next chapter, we will spend some time exploring what activities can generate an online income.

Language teachers, yoga teachers and dive instructors are some of the professions that allow you to visit awe-inspiring places, and freely move among them. In fact, many of the current digital nomads have come from the 'analog nomad' world. They had already been living and working overseas, when they saw an influx of digital nomads who made them rethink their career choice. Some of these old-school nomads chose to combine a more traditional job abroad, while experimenting with online activities. Once their online income hits a safe and consistent level, they may opt out of their old career and into a truly location-independent one.

FIND YOUR SWEET SPOT

It's surprising how many people have no idea what they're good at, let alone how to make money as an entrepreneur. On the other hand, many digital nomads' minds are racing with business ideas. You may have so many ideas that you feel paralyzed – you don't know which one to pick. Whatever the reason you haven't succeeded so far, the best way to overcome this barrier is to identify your added value, and find ways to turn that into an income. Often, it's something you've considered as a weakness up to now, or a trait you aren't even aware of, that makes you special.

Natalie Sisson, famous in digital nomad circles for her bestseller and blog (suitcaseentrepreneur.com), believes that you should pick the one idea that is right in the intersection of what you're passionate about, what you're good at, and what people are willing to pay for (see page 194).

Often, you discover a skill or business idea by doing something completely unrelated. Esther collected all leftover foreign coins for charity, when the Euro was introduced in the Netherlands in 2002. She eventually raised €16 million and got a lot of publicity. While she initiated 'Coins for Care' as a charity project –she did not get paid– she learned a lot and got to know many 'famous' people in business, politics, and the media, and they got to notice her. Afterward, companies asked Esther to give presentations about 'achieving big results with few resources'. Before she knew it, she was a well-paid speaker at business conferences. By constantly reinventing herself, and turning everything that happened in her life into a key-note speech (even participating in the reality show Survivor and a love affair with a 'Mr. Wrong'), she has been able to make a living as a speaker for over 15 years now. Since audiences kept asking her for a book, she wrote 'What is your excuse?', and several other Dutch bestsellers. She discovered a very easy and fast way to write books, and started teaching and helping others in her workshops: 'How to Write Your Book in a Week', in exotic locations. Who would have thought that a charity project could lead to a life where people pay you to do and talk about what you love?

Tal Gur (page 157) started a blog out of enthusiasm for his favorite country, Australia. He now makes a six-figure income from running a number of similar websites.

Laura Viviana found that she loves writing and that she's really good at it. She is now a high-end copywriter, travelling the world. More about Laura on page 186.

RESULTS

No idea where to start? Esther is really good at identifying and communicating someone's' essence, or 'personal branding', as it is sometimes called. In one RESULTant session, she helps you define your unique selling point and a fitting slogan. In another session, she could help you structure your website, define products around your theme and helps you to write the content for the main pages.

 bit.ly/resultant-session

FOUR WAYS TO MAKE MONEY ONLINE

There are basically four categories in which you can make a living on the internet.

1) Having a remote job means that you work for a boss and enjoy a steady income. Instead of going to an office, you work remotely and take care of your own workplace, whether that's at home or on the road. You may be required to be connected at certain hours of the day, or may have to come into the office a number of times a year.

2) As a freelancer, you make a living one project at a time. Clients hire you for a coaching session, a business plan, to have a new website made, to have a personal training plan drawn up, or to have music composed, just to name a few examples. You typically deliver 'sessions' or services by deadlines, after which you get paid.

3) Create a passive income with an online business. Instead of exchanging hours for remuneration, the ultimate challenge is to set up a business that generates money by itself. Of course, there is still work involved, but the number of hours worked is not directly related to the income generated.

4) As an investor, you let your money work for you. This can be done as a foreign exchange trader, or as an angel investor in new technologies. You could even sublet your house, either long-term or through Airbnb, or become a full-fledged property investor.

You can stay exclusively within one of these categories or choose to combine two or more categories, which is what many digital nomads do. An example would be a freelancer, who is also setting up his own online business, or a remote worker who does freelance work for third parties.

In this chapter, we will take a look at each one of these options and the plethora of activities that can be done within each category. From the obvious to the surprising, chances are, you will find an activity that best suits your talents and experience.

I) GET A REMOTE JOB

A remote job combines the certainty of a monthly salary with the freedom of location-independence. Yes, you have a job, contract and a boss, but you don't have to commute to his office every day. Depending on the work, you may be required to drop in once in a while, or you may never even meet face-to-face.

What started out as a perk for workers with children is slowly, but surely, revolutionizing the way offices organize their work. The infrastructure is in place; we have internet and phones and daycare. It's a matter of trust now, as far as bosses are concerned. Bosses who do trust their workers to work remotely report increased productivity and lower absenteeism.

Changing to remote work also requires managers to think in terms of output rather than input. Do they really want a worker to be connected eight hours a day, the same way a worker was expected to be in the office eight hours a day? And how would he check this? It would be better to set goals and work toward them.

WORK FROM HOME

If you already have an office job, but your boss seems reluctant to let you work remotely, Timothy Ferriss gives some useful tips in his bestseller, The Four Hour Work Week. Ask if you can work from home one day a week, as a trial, for a month or two, after which you and your boss would evaluate future remote opportunities. The 'mistake' most people make, when working from home, is reading reports and other stuff for which they need focus and quiet time, which they don't get in the office. However, this makes you virtually invisible during the days you are not working in the office. Ferriss recommends that you do your 'most visible work' from home. Prepare emails and reports at the office, but send them from home on your 'work-at-home day'. Do your reading at the office. Make sure your boss can quantify your productivity after the agreed period.

Then ask for an additional day to work from home. As long as your boss cannot deny your (increased) productivity, you stand a better chance at achieving the perfect work/life balance.

In Berlin we met a girl from latin America, who worked for Fiverr's customer service. She was required to log in eight hours per day and resolve a certain number of 'tickets'. Otherwise, she was free to work from whatever location she liked. She had a good salary ($3,000+ per month), which she chose to spend in 'cheap' countries. She would move to a new city every two months, live in Airbnb apartments, and work from coffee shops. A perfect combination of the security of a job, and the freedom of a nomad.

WHERE TO FIND REMOTE JOBS
Tech-based companies seem to be the front-runners when it comes to remote work. Many start-ups are made up entirely of so-called 'distributed teams' that work across time zones. Their founders and workers communicate through email, chat on Slack and hold videoconferences through Google Hangouts (more about productivity tools on page 231. If you are looking for a remote job, these would be your dream employers.

Regularly check the website of companies working with distributed teams, such as:
* Basecamp.com
* Buffer.com
* MailerLite.com
* Fiverr.com
* Automattic.com

A job board that focuses on remote work at tech companies is remoteok.io
Non-techies would do better to check out Flexjobs: flexjobs.com

2) BECOME A FREELANCER

Don't feel like being tied to a work contract? As a freelancer, you have more freedom. You work on a project basis for different clients, which usually means you can organize your time around your travels, or your most productive hours.

One of your main challenges will be to get clients. Info and tips on page 202. You can also join an agency to get jobs. Upwork.com (previously Elance) connects organizations and projects with freelancers from all over the world.

Being a freelancer means that your income will fluctuate. There will be months you rake in thousands of euros, and there will be months that you can hardly scrape by. Some freelancers negotiate long-term contracts to get get a bit more grip on these fluctuations. By spreading your work for a client over the whole year, instead of concentrating it in a short term burst, you enjoy a base income that will grow with the number of long-term clients you're able to score. Whether you want to call it a maintenance agreement, or a campaign, will depend on the type of freelance work you do. For example, an SEO professional cannot only offer a one-time website optimization, but can include continual monitoring of website rankings, and offer periodic optimization efforts, at a monthly or annual fee.

Another way to stabilize a freelance income is by 'productizing' your services, which basically entails that you pre-package your services and make a compelling offer. For example, if you're an SEO copywriter, you can offer a 'website check' for €99, or a series of 10 blog posts for €499. Productized services help clients to get a better sense of what they buy; they are more credible, easier to replicate (and thus easier to outsource), and the fixed prices prevent clients from trying to get a discount.

Examples of freelance jobs:

⭐ **Website and/or webshop builder**
If you can build a simple WordPress site in a free template, you already know more than 99% of the world, meaning that you can help others get their (first?) website up, and get paid for it. Watch a few tutorials on YouTube, build a website for yourself, and you're in business. Add a standard web shop to the template and you can help anybody start their business. Learn on the job, or get a 'coach' like Marika Porrey (web-sidekick.com) who teaches you the more difficult steps via Skype. Marika offers to give you free feedback and tips on improving your (online business) website.

⭐ **Internet marketer**
From community management to setting up pay-per-click ad campaigns for clients, internet marketing is a wide domain with a low barrier to entry. There are tons of blogs out there that will teach you how to work the different channels to make a website easier to find, or how to optimize web pages for conversion (e.g. sales). SmartPassiveIncome.com is one such blog, renowned for Pat Flynn's patient and personal approach.

⭐ **Copywriter**
A copywriter is not someone who works with patents and copyright. The term actually refers to writing copy; copy being the content that is placed in ads, brochures, on websites, and in other promotional media. One branch of copywriting is SEO copywriting. SEO is an abbreviation for Search Engine Optimization, and SEO copy helps a website to get the best rankings for certain keywords. It may sound very technical, but anyone who has a way with words can learn this job. André has a course that teaches would-be SEO copywriters the ropes: beachwriter.net

Language teacher

Teaching English as a foreign language (TEFL) is a proven way to see the world. You can sign a work contract with a foreign language school and move to that country, thus converting into an 'analog nomad', or you can teach students online. Thanks to Skype or Google Hangouts, you can connect to students anywhere in the world. One strategy is to find students yourself, for example, through a blog and social media chattering. Another option, great for teachers who are just starting out, is teaching through a platform. Most schools require TEFL or other certificates. Platforms may only ask for a test video to approve your language level.

On NiceTalk.com you can earn $10 per hour teaching English to Chinese students. Myngle.com allows anyone to teach his or her native language, or any other language they speak fluently. iTalki.com and verbalplanet.com are other popular teaching sites.

Programmer

Developers, programmers, and coders love solving the 'puzzles' that clients create for them. Many of them work on their own projects too, creating software, as a service (SaaS), or mobile apps.

Photographer

Every photographer's dream is being sent on assignment (preferably accompanied by a journalist), by a magazine or other publication. Most of the time, though, he or she will be doing small local jobs and/or creating and selling his/her own projects. Remember that your website is your 'shopping window', so display your favorite work to attract similar projects, not what you think will sell best. A way to create a passive income is to sell pictures on stock photo websites. While these marketplaces pay only a few cents per photo sold, they enjoy a lot of traffic, which means a photo can be sold again and again.

✹ Coach

If you are really good at something, you can help others. You don't have to know everything, or be the best. As long as you know a bit more than your clients, you can help them with their next step. Sometimes, just listening and asking logical questions is all a person needs. Milana Leshinksy (milana.com) offers great guidance on how to become a coach and how to leverage your business into a passive income stream.

Tips from an experienced freelancer on how to find clients, and tips especially on what NOT to do: bit.ly/freelancer-finding-clients

Laura Viviana (1983) traveled a lot in her early twenties, and then found a dream job as a copywriter on Wall Street. So how did she end up across the table from Esther in Southeast Asia? In this interview, Laura openly shares her journey, ups and downs and learnings. And indeed, she has a way with words...

Life's glorious changes often start with loss and shock—mine was no different. My journey to full-time expat status started on a chilly NYC night in March, when I came home to my beloved partner from a dear friend's funeral. The night ended with me throwing books at the wall: he broke up with me, I never saw it coming, and 6 months of intense heartache ensued. I sobbed in subways and in cemeteries on my lunch break from my cubicle position—which, to be fair, helped me keep it together when I sorely needed stability. I was in shock: the future I had envisioned for myself was now a blank road into an unknown horizon. Little did I know that my ex's brave decision to follow his heart would crack open my chance to live in communion with my highest good.

In trying to accept that my life—my title at a prestigious publishing firm, my sunny, wood-floored Brooklyn apartment, my loving relationship—was no longer the life I truly wanted, I sought refuge in meditation (my life's constant companion), trusted advisors, and wine. Just kidding. In actuality, I felt through my pain with determined lucidity and sobriety. After listening to what my heart really wanted, I bought my ticket, kissed my mom's forehead, and hopped on a plane— alone.

That was roughly two years ago at the time of this writing. I've continued this lifestyle in Southeast Asia, South America, and Australasia. While my online visibility is only a few years old, I've actually been freelancing for eight years, so I've hit that "tipping-point" that happens after building a solid client base: most of my clients come to me through referral. I didn't know that was going to be the case when I started this journey, but when I took the dive into my new life, things really did fall into place. But please take heart if this all sounds like a fairytale: mine is not an overnight success story! I'm happy for that. I've earned where I am, and much of my success is due to years of building my business before I took the flight into the unknown. It's not a linear process, and I did fail.

About that. "Failure to fly" actually happened way before my NYC breakdown and subsequent rising; throughout my teens and twenties I lived in South America, Europe, and New Zealand— studying, WOOFING and taking weird jobs to make ends meet. Even after I started my business, I tried fully freelancing and moved to the Deep South of America, where I completely crashed and burned. I just wasn't ready yet, and needed a few more years of polishing before I could take the big jump into digital nomadship. So remember: journeys are winding and unpredictable—but as long as you follow your gut and senses, you'll get to where you're going. It's vitally important to appreciate where you are, right now, so you can passionately move towards where you want to be.

Back to the present: there's much to love about living abroad. On a practical level, prices are much more affordable and the standard of living is higher per dollar. This is excellent for people who are just starting out with freelancing, or don't have a stable income. While living abroad I've been able to save for my pension, create a sizable emergency net of cash, and become financially fluent in ways that I didn't have to be in America. There's also the freedom of living without a lot of "stuff"! At the moment, I don't own much but I do have a tremendously expansive life; the freedom to live how I choose.

I try to stay low-key and humble about the lifestyle I maintain, but in the interest of honesty, I'll divulge: it's fabulous. Depending on where

I am, I often have access to a personal chef, a personal masseuse, daily housekeeping, and personal training. My access to incredible exotic destinations and "workcations" is fantastic. I always dreamed of becoming an anthropologist, so being near radically different cultures leaves me in constant amazement and respect. Motorbiking is like meditation to me—I do it as often as I can. Expat communities are more thriving than ever, and I've made some dear friends.

Here's where I'm going to slay the dreamy bubble I've just crafted for you: sustainable nomadship requires a tremendous amount of responsibility. I must be vigilant about always having the right travel insurance, the right visa, maintaining apartments in multiple countries, and being financially aware. I work with a trusted accountant, and have a business coach who guides me—the truth is that nobody does this kind of thing alone! We need professionals and support systems to help us along.

I'm usually traveling alone most of the time, so I'm extremely street-smart and careful about how I live my life: safety and wellness are big priorities. Getting sick with parasites or typhoid are common in developing countries, so I make sure that my immune system is prepared to deal with anything at any moment. For me, that means no heavy partying or neglecting my nutrition; I simply can't get away with reckless living or skipping out on exercising and meditating. It's not sexy or glamorous, but it's the truth. (Ok, so maybe if my favorite DJ is in town I'll break my rules—life is short!)

As a creative writer and poet, living outside of America has been paramount to my artistic growth. Being able to see oneself outside of the context you're accustomed to is both scary and an incredible gift. My creative work and self-realization have soared since beginning to travel. As well, I've learned how to take normally crazy situations in stride and with a calm attitude. I've climbed way out of my comfort zone living abroad, and I'm much stronger now. In general, this way of living helps me to feel passionately alive and constantly challenged.

The main drawback of being an expat is missing my family and friends when I'm far away. The distance makes me live very deliberately, and I find myself putting a lot of deep thought into prioritization of loved ones, and how to balance my freedom with "showing up" for them. My yearly travel plans always revolve around putting my family first. Maintaining deep friendships and connections as one gets older becomes an important act—like tending a garden.

On the other hand, being a freelancer allows me to spend more time with my family per year than the average two weeks that most American salaried employees have. To me, trying to decide whether or not you'll vacation or go see your family during those time off is an unkind, no-win situation. This year I spent most of the summer with my friends and family; I took my mom on a spa vacation, and hiked a bunch with my dad. I love that running my own business allows me to be the kind of family member I want to be, and that if anything were to happen to someone I care about, I could be with them without fear of losing my job.

Some digital nomads I meet are big partiers and get caught in escaping from the actual responsibility of living. That might be fun for a while, but I've met a lot of people who either burn out or get into trouble that way. Let's face it—being reckless when you're abroad is a big gamble. Of course, everyone has their own journey, but I don't recommend being irresponsible if you're trying to run a serious business.

Above all: I believe that the remote business owners and entrepreneurs of today are shaping our world of tomorrow: we're paving the way for others. We are the pioneers. For me, I take that very seriously. I'm focused on not falling into the "neo-colonialism" trap of altering a place to suit my Western needs—which ends up changing entire economies and sometimes exploiting citizens. I make sure I know a culture and respect it as I'm exploring it; I remember that for many people, I represent 'America.' If I can be compassionate, respectful, and open to what others have to teach me, then in my own small way I'm bringing about understanding and peace. In short, I feel grateful that I'm able to live this way, and I don't take that for granted.

Laura's tips:

Don't leave home without some kind of an 'insurance'. Always have enough money at hand, or a credit card you can use to fly back home if needed. But be reasonable about it—don't let a lack of a whole year's salary in your savings account stop you. Travel insurance is a must.

Try the digital nomad lifestyle with a safety opt-out. Some people are totally sure that this is for them, and some people aren't. If it's all new to you, or if you are worried, choose a starting country that is not too far away. It also really helps to have some sort of 'anchor' in a country before you get there. It might be volunteering, a job, or some sort of a community. This helps you ease into the culture and lifestyle, so you don't feel lost. I find it grounding to have contacts in a country and be involved in something organized in a new country.

Remember that this road is rich and rewarding—but also winding! It's not like becoming a doctor where the steps are laid out and you have tons of peer support and whole institutions to guide you. There are times when you will feel hopeless or scared because you've chosen a very different path—embrace that fear because it's all part of this lifestyle. Reach out to other people like yourself, make sure to be responsible, take very good care of yourself, and you'll be okay. In fact, you'll probably be better than you ever imagined. ☺

 www.lauraviviana.com

3) CREATE A PASSIVE INCOME WITH AN ONLINE BUSINESS

We work to live, instead of living to work. Digital nomad life is really about freedom, and you can't get more of that until you free up some time. For example by moving on from a job or freelance career to start your own company and generate passive income. That's right – you'll need to become an entrepreneur if you want to stop trading hours for money. Robert Kiyosaki, author of Rich Dad, Poor Dad, drew up his famous cash flow quadrant to show 'the preferred route' to financial independence. In other words, to freedom.

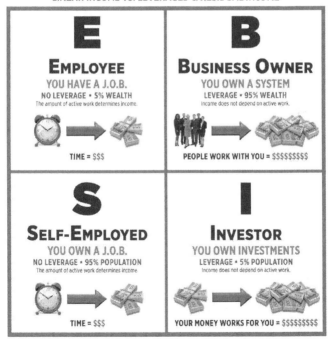

CASHFLOW QUADRANT

4 WAYS TO PRODUCE INCOME
LINEAR INCOME VS. LEVERAGED & RESIDUAL INCOME

E

EMPLOYEE
YOU HAVE A J.O.B.
NO LEVERAGE • 5% WEALTH
The amount of active work determines income.

TIME = $$$

B

BUSINESS OWNER
YOU OWN A SYSTEM
LEVERAGE • 95% WEALTH
Income does not depend on active work.

PEOPLE WORK WITH YOU = $$$$$$$$$

S

SELF-EMPLOYED
YOU OWN A J.O.B.
NO LEVERAGE • 95% POPULATION
The amount of active work determines income.

TIME = $$$

I

INVESTOR
YOU OWN INVESTMENTS
LEVERAGE • 5% POPULATION
Income does not depend on active work.

YOUR MONEY WORKS FOR YOU = $$$$$$$$$

Source: bit.ly/cashflow-quad

There seems to be a fine line between a freelancer and an entrepreneur. And indeed, many freelancers will argue that they are entrepreneurs – after all, they run a business. One similarity is that both are responsible for their own success. Also, they set their own work hours, have clients, need to hire help when necessary, and have to file their own taxes. The difference, however, is as subtle as it is important. One is time-independent and the other isn't. A freelancer gets paid by the hour or project, and has a certain work capacity (since there are only 24 hours in a day). He is only paid when he works, and the only thing he can do to raise his income is by working more hours or raising his rates. An entrepreneur builds a business with leverage; he aims to take on more clients, or sell more products, irrespective of the work hours he puts in.

Entrepreneurs use money to build a business bigger than themselves so that they can get paid when they sleep. They focus on growth and on scaling the systems that they build. The more, the better.
– Seth Godin –

The popular term 'passive income' is deceiving. "Invest your time and money once and then lean back to see the sales, commission, or royalties roll in," as advertized on various internet marketing platforms. The fact of the matter is, even the smartest system is still hands-on and will require maintenance or upgrading. In addition, there's a lot of competition.

André experienced this when he started publishing Kindle ebooks in 2012. He didn't write them himself; he hired freelancers to write the e-books and design the covers. André owned the rights to the books, which meant that he made between $0.30 and $5.60 per ebook sale.

After about a year, he had 20+ e-books in the Amazon Kindle Store, with monthly royalties around $2,000. "That income made my trip through Central America a lot more comfortable! However, I spent too much time enjoying the royalties, and too little time promoting my books, or publishing new books. After a few months, the monthly income from Kindle sales had crumbled to about $100 a month." What was presented as a passive income system wasn't so passive, after all.

Two approaches to creating passive income
a) Turn something you really like, which you are really good at, into a digital product.
b) Find a service or product in a popular category and sell it in a web shop. These are usually physical products.

In both cases you will need a web shop. This can either be your own shop or an existing platform such as Amazon, eBay or similar sites. The great thing about visitors to a web shop is that everyone has the intention to buy – either right now, or in the future. It's your job to seduce these visitors with a beautiful design, attractive prices, and social proof. And good products, of course.

a) Sell digital products
One of the most viable ways of making a location-independent living is by selling digital products. They can be your own, or somebody else's:

* E-books
* Online courses
* Music downloads
* Podcasts
* Audiobooks
* Software
* Webinars
* Video tutorials
* (Stock)photos

Only the initial creation of the product takes time and/or money; the cost price of each extra product you sell is zero (except for marketing). You don't need a physical storage place, payment can be taken by a third party (PayPal, Ideal, credit card, etc. More info about payment systems on page 34), and the delivery can be fully automated. This means that you can create your income anywhere and around the clock, e.g. make money even while you sleep or laze on a tropical beach.

Esther first published her books via the biggest publishing house in the Netherlands. In 2009, they chose to only produce physical books. When Esther also wanted a digital version of her books, she had to make it herself. Because there were a lot of illustrations in the books, she couldn't turn them into proper e-books (epub), so she settled for PDF. Many of her readers use tablets, so that was a good enough solution. She offered her e-books in her own web shop: a simple plugin to her WordPress website. Soon, she was making a few hundred euros each month without making any extra effort. Getting an automated email with a copy of the sale of a €6,95 ebook in the Netherlands is nice, but getting the same email in Bali, Indonesia, means her readers bought her dinner that evening ☺.

NATALIE SISSONS' 3 STEPS TO FINDING YOUR SWEET SPOT
Step 1: What do you love doing?
You know yourself better than anyone. Make a list of all the things you enjoy doing. List as many things as possible, for example: dancing, cooking, painting, writing, speaking, solving IT problems, throwing parties, editing proposals, finding sponsors, pouring coffees, or advising people on their next move.

Step 2: What are you good at?
There are probably a lot of things you enjoy doing, but maybe you don't think anybody would ever pay you for it. One solution is to ask your friends and co-workers what you're good at. You'll often

find that they see something in you that you have never considered. Maybe it's something that comes naturally to you, but you don't see it as a skill set.

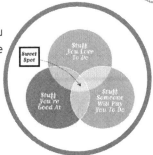

Step 3: What will people pay you for?
Next is finding the love/skill matches for which there is a market. Now, if I were a pretty bad French cook, and you made French-cooking seem easy and approachable and friendly, then I would probably pay you to teach me how to be a better French cook.

What your business could look like
Just get out your iPhone, get a microphone, and start doing You-Tube videos of you preparing a French meal, making it super simple and fun and entertaining. That part is your free content. You can then have it transcribed and turn it into a written guidebook. You can start creating recipe books that people will actually pay you 10 or 20 dollars at a time for.

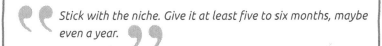

> *Stick with the niche. Give it at least five to six months, maybe even a year.*

Don't stop there! You can progress into products and programs, for example, a 5-week online cooking class, taking students from one point to being an expert French cook. Then you can produce a book. Maybe you can even go on TV and talk about your passion and how you have helped busy stay-at-home mums to become incredible French cooks.

Natalie Sisson helps online entrepreneurs create a profitable business. **More info:**

 suitcaseentrepreneur.com

♭) Sell physical products

Imagine finding the perfect gadget in China, or handmade traditional bags in Peru. You know the world needs these... It would be even better to check the best selling categories on the worlds largest marketplace Amazon.com and actively look for a suitable product on Alibaba.com, where Chinese producers offer their products.

Your product doesn't need to be world changing. Many bestsellers are in the household or pet products categories. For example, one of the current bestsellers is a life vest for chickens... Seriously!

There are many online courses about selling on Amazon and sourcing products from Asia. Just a few practical tips:

★ Don't sell electronic products. Chances are some of them won't work and you would need a return- and customer service. Same for breakable products: don't do it!

★ Pick products in the best selling categories.

★ Check similar products on Amazon: how are your competitors presenting and pricing them?

★ Make sure you have great pictures and copy to present your product

★ Use a separate email address for Alibaba.com: you will receive lots of spam.

★ Appear professional when approaching suppliers: don't let them know you are just starting out.

- Request various sample products to compare quality. Sometimes you have to pay for a sample, but this is worth it. Often the sample payment is deducted from your final order.
- Minimum order quantities (MOQ) are negotiable.
- Prices are negotiable.
- You can brand your products by having your logo printed on them. Ask for pictures of other branded products to see what the product looks like with print.
- Check everything: the quality of the product, quantity in the boxes etc. There are even professional checking companies in the areas of the biggest manufacturers that you can hire to do this.
- Amazon requires that each product be labeled with a separate unique ISBN number or bar code. You can buy these barcodes online. The producer will stick them onto each product if you email them the barcode.
- Get reviews for your product a.s.a.p. Either from friends and family or by offering a review product in a special Facebook group or at a discount.

You'd think that selling physical products require a physical warehouse, with employees who pick orders and prepare products for shipment. And yes, even an online store requires this, but it doesn't have to be you who runs the warehouse. It doesn't even have to be you who holds the stock. Instead, a fulfillment company will be happy to reserve space for your products and ship them out to your customers. Your fulfillment company will even tell you when the batch of products is running out and when a new one should be ordered. In return, these companies take a percentage of your sales, charge a monthly fee or per product fee, or sometimes a combination of these. Amazon.com also offers fulfillment services. Everything comes at a price, though, so do your research.

A similar option – but less risky – is selling goods through drop shipping. You do not keep any goods in stock; rather, you transfer customer orders and shipment details to either the manufacturer, another retailer, or a wholesaler, who then ships the goods directly to your customer. This doesn't require you to buy and store a minimum number of products. You promote products that somebody else produces, stores and sends to your customers. All you have to do is tell them where to send which product and they will pay you a commission per sale.

This is similar to affiliate marketing. Did you know that you can, for example, offer books and other products from Amazon.com on your website, and receive a percentage of the turnover that is generated from your 'affiliate link'? The trick is not to just offer everything, but to make a good selection that really complements your content. For example, you can link to all the products you need to make the recipes on your blog, or all the management books you recommend about a specific topic. Write a short review about each product or book on your site or blog, with an affiliate link to Amazon.

CJ.com and Clickbank.com are two of the biggest affiliate networks. Affili.net and Zanox.com are big European networks. These sites offer thousands of services and products that you can promote on your own website, to your newsletter subscribers, or your YouTube viewers.

4) LET YOUR MONEY WORK FOR YOU

The most revered way of making money is having your money work for you, by investing it in physical, financial, or digital assets. Please note that this is also the most risky and therefore specialized way. So research well and make sure to get expert advice. Some basic guidelines from our experts and digital nomads:

Investing in stock or bonds

You invest through various online platforms, have your bank take care of it, or invest in a combined fund for better results. Whatever you do: use your common sense and keep it simple. If it sounds too good to be true, it probably is. Complicated products were invented to make the bank a lot of money, not you. Focus on bonds or stock and don't get into hedge funds, private equity, derivates, commodities or infrastructure.

Bonds: Nowadays we live in a 'low return environment' because the interest rate is very low and is likely to remain so. This makes it difficult to make much money with government bonds. In some cases, the interest rate on government bonds is even negative (e.g. Denmark and Switzerland). That means you can earn more by investing in corporate bonds. You take a little more risk because the issuer is not a government but a business, but you're still relatively safe if you invest in investment grade corporate bonds. You can also choose riskier high-yield bonds. The probability of default is a bit higher but the yield is also higher. Government bonds have a yield of say 2% and you get a risk premium if you choose corporate bonds. Right now you get around 4% for investment grade corporate bonds. Invest in bonds mainly for the income/yield and not for capital appreciation.

Equities: this asset class is riskier than bonds, so the equity risk premium is higher than that for bonds. But the upside is greater than for bonds, because you can get hefty price increases. Shares are bought mainly for capital appreciation and not for the income. You can opt for emerging markets (Latam, Asia) which are more risky than (over-) developed markets (such as Europe and the US). It's better to stick to the markets you know well.

Funds vs. individual securities: It's tempting to invest in individual stocks or credits, but as an individual you do not have the resources to analyze annual reports. Therefore it's better to go for funds that give you diversification across a large number of names.

Active vs. passive: you can invest in actively managed funds, but you will probably pay a percent and most research demonstrated that passive funds do equally well. For passive funds you probably pay 0.1% so you're much better off.

In what currency should your investments be? Currencies are notoriously difficult to predict, so as a private investor you shouldn't even try. It is always good to spread your assets, so have some in dollars, some in euros etc. The rule of thumb is that your assets should match your liabilities. So if your costs are largely in Euros you have to invest most of your assets in Europe.

Trading platforms: since we live in a low return environment, costs are now more important than ever. If you earn 4% in the market but have to pay 2.5% to advisors, asset managers, trading commissions etc., then there's only 1.5% left. And a fee of 2.5% has become more the rule than an exception, even though you're often not told. The best is to work without expensive brokers or asset managers and invest through low cost trading platforms, like TDAmeritrade.com and Scottrade.com in the US, Hargreaves Lansdown (hl.co.uk) and Nutmeg.com in the UK and Alex.nl of Binck.com in the Netherlands.

Diversification: it is essential to spread your assets. Diversification is the only free lunch in finance; meaning you should not put all your eggs in one basket. So buy some stocks and bonds (financial assets) but also invest in a house (real assets). And buy your shares and assets in different currencies, so your risk is spread in various ways.

Business angel

Some nomads travel the world in search of great ideas to invest in. These so-called business angels visit trade fairs and attend 'demo days', where startups pitch for funding. Some take a more active role in a start-up with a solid exit strategy. "I've sold two businesses now, which was like selling mini houses," says Jon Yongfook in the (upcoming) documentary One Way Ticket (digitalnomaddocumentary.com). "I think it's perfectly possible to build up digital assets in the same way that you build physical assets. I guess I look at it in the same way as investing in a property, but it's just a lot more flexible."

Real estate and trading

Others focus on real estate, either buying properties to rent out short term (Airbnb) or longer term (for example, to ex-pats), or they 'flip' properties for profit.

Digital nomads Rob & Mish, who run the excellent blog Makingitanywhere.com, own and manage various properties in the UK, and run a real estate podcast.

Ina Wessels used to be a nurse in The Netherlands. When she found out about tax liens in the USA, she started trading in those 'tax claims on houses', and later buying actual houses in auctions and selling them at a profit. She managed to grow her modest starting capital and now, five years later, she is traveling the world while earning an income with tax liens. She also presents workshops and sells online courses to others who are interested: taxliens.eu

This guide is principally aimed at nomads who wish to minimize their financial risks. That's why we will focus on the first three categories: remote jobs, freelance work, and online businesses.

MAKE CLIENTS COME TO YOU

One of the challenges of being an independent contractor, free-lancer, or entrepreneur, is attracting and closing clients. Especially if you're just starting out, this may seem a constant struggle, in comparing yourself to established and more experienced remote employees, freelancers, and businesses. Don't let others discourage you; you can't control what they do; all you can do is control your own attitude, work, and image. Find your own added value and focus on being visible, so clients can find you.

SHOW YOUR ADDED VALUE

Cold calling, cold emailing, or competing with freelancers in online contests can be frustrating. Wouldn't it be better if clients came to you of their own accord? You can be great at what you do, but if nobody knows you exist, you won't get any (new) clients.

Pat Flynn's 'Be Everywhere' approach on smartpassiveincome.com/how-to-be-everywhere/ is a good way to reach potential clients. It entails creating valuable content, and sharing it across the biggest social networks. Not only content for your own website, but also for others, for example, as a guest blogger. That way, you can build a list of followers and newsletter subscribers who will think about you first whenever they have a relevant project.

Think of your website, blog, newsletter, social media, etc. as your 'shopping window'. Display those items you would like to be seen, the areas you would like to work at, and the things you are good at – not just a list of all the things you have done in the past. Make sure your website is optimized with the right keywords (SEO), and the bios of your various social media channels are consistent. Use various social media channels (Facebook, Twitter, Pinterest, Instagram, Youtube, etc.) for different sorts of posts. Share your photos, music, video's, quotes, humor, insights, interesting websites, news items; whatever is relevant to who you are, what you do, and how you can help others. Instead of thinking of sales, focus on sharing your personality, insights, experiences and inspiration.

It's not just about pushing your content all the time, which may come across as spammy. Engage with your (potential) clients, follow them on Twitter, give advice, share interesting articles and crack the odd joke on Facebook. If you are prepared to invest in your visibility and if you are patient, you will be rewarded with more clients than you can handle.

WEBSITE
Whether you plan to make your online income by blogging or by selling t-shirts, you will need your own little place on the internet. A catchy domain name – or even your own name as the URL– is the starting point. After this, many nomads choose to build their websites on the WordPress platform (more info on page 234), which now accounts for 25% of all websites on the internet. Be sure to invest in a reliable, flexible host, with strict security measures (see page 61). It would be a shame if your passive income stream dried up due to a hack or an error message due to too many page views.

PORTFOLIO
Would you hire someone if you were not sure of his or her work quality? Would you pay someone without knowing what you're getting? When adopting the client's point of view, it makes perfect sense to look for digital nomads who are proud of their earlier work. And even if your style or price doesn't match the client's desires, he may still refer you to someone else who needs a hand. In short, not having a portfolio is a missed chance every time a potential client visits your website.

Use what you have, make your archives accessible through your website. Some people mistakenly assume that a portfolio can only contain paid assignments. If you are just starting out, it is perfectly acceptable to include personal, charity, or university projects, links to media appearances, and references.

If photo, audio, or video files are quite large, consider not storing them on your own site (you will have to pay for more server space), but using free services available instead. Esther had an assistant digitize her media archive; she keeps all radio interviews on Sound-Cloud.com, TV interviews and other videos on YouTube, and magazine and newspaper articles on Scribd.com. You can either link to or embed each item on your website, without having to store the original file there.

SOCIAL MEDIA

Your social media posts enable others to see how you experience the world. They might conclude that you have original ideas, write well, take amazing pictures, have a sense of humor, or are able to connect with others, just to name a few. It might not lead directly to a sale, but in the long run they'll remember you and won't hesitate to contact you when they need you(r services).

Many people are insecure about what to post. Try to focus on a certain topic and find different media, like music, cartoons, pictures, quotes, and links about your theme. When you read an article that might interest your contacts, don't just post it, but include a comment or observation (what is so good/special about it?), or post a question. Share eye openers and answer frequently asked questions, instead of just promoting yourself.

The great thing about social media is that you get immediate feedback. If you are losing Twitter followers, you should evaluate the content you posted. The number of likes, and especially shares, on Facebook gives you an idea about the popularity of your posts. Klout.com measures your influence. If your work has anything to do with (social) media, clients might look up your Klout score, so you'd better check it regularly yourself.

EMAIL LIST

Next to social media and blog posts, you still want to collect email addresses of your contacts. Nothing beats a direct email to your clients, but only if you use your list wisely. Share information and tips that are interesting to your readers. Offer them links to more background info. Links will land you more visitors, which, in turn, can result in more sales. Monitoring the so-called open rates for emails, and the subsequent click-through rates, will give you more insight on the interests of your readers. What's more, the luxury of reaching thousands of followers with a mouse click is unprecedented. Did you know that many marketers are still banging their heads against the wall for not collecting email addresses from the beginning?

If you're not building an email list, you're an idiot.
– Derek Halpern, marketer and entrepreneur (socialtriggers.com) –

Popular services for sending newsletters to lists of people are Mailchimp.com and AWeber.com. There are some subtle differences in features and pricing. This blogpost does a good job of comparing the two services: bit.ly/mailchimp-aweber

IT'S NOT ABOUT YOU!

Many websites, newsletters, and social media posts are about the sender. "We have landed this new project." "We are proud to present our new website.", "I am on my way to a client.", etc. Always think about the receiver first; what does he/she gain from this text, post, or message? Your newsletter should not be about what your company has done in the past months, rather about a certain theme that affects your clients. Share everything you come across that might be useful or inspiring to your audience. Don't think about sales, think about connecting and sharing. Start your website pages with a client's question, and answer it, instead of listing your CV. By generating user-relevant content, you will get more results that last longer.

WALK THE TALK

Everything you do, both while working and in your private time, should be consistent. Would Esther be credible as a motivational speaker if she had never actually achieved anything herself? The €16 million she raised for charity makes her an authority on 'achieving more results with few resources' and 'out of the box' thinking. If André offers SEO courses, but his own website ranks depressingly low, would he be taken seriously?

I was ecstatic! I had finally reached the number 1 spot in Google for the Dutch version of 'SEO copywriter'. What better way was there to prove that I could improve someone's search engine rankings? I walked the talk and clients were beating a path to my Inbox.

How I managed to get my top ranking? I didn't need to hire sketchy link builders or stuff my site with keywords, but simply wrote articles and columns for big online publications. They didn't pay me, but they did link back to my website, which helped build authority.

Ideally, you could do the same if you were just starting out. Find an online newspaper or industry-related blog and offer to contribute. Try to get paid, but don't despair if it's 'link juice' instead of money that they offer. You will be paid back in clients in the long run.

– André Gussekloo –

In order to achieve this consistency, don't just think about making money. Freely share your knowledge, in order to build your image and create an online following. Make sure your actions on social media don't contradict your image. If you coach people to stop smoking, but your Facebook photos show you puffing away, that won't help.

HOW TO PRESENT YOURSELF AND/OR YOUR COMPANY

Whether you're looking to find clients, hire a freelancer, or hook up with a business partner, there are many factors that influence your success. If you're lacking in one factor, you can compensate for this by emphasizing other strong points. Most importantly, find your own authentic way of doing business. You might lose some clients who don't connect with that, but the clients you do attract will appreciate you for who you are and how you work.

MIND YOUR ATTITUDE

Did you contact your potential client or did he get in touch first? If you took the initiative, you may very well be rewarded for your pro-active attitude. Your enthusiasm is a sign that you will pour your heart into your work. On the other hand, some clients mistake enthusiasm for desperate. If you are known for your good work, you may never have to look for clients again; they will come to you, through word of mouth, or your website. Not actively looking for clients might actually get you some!

YOUR LOCATION CAN BE A SELLING POINT

Let's face it, some clients prefer to work with employees, freelancers, or businesses in their own town or region, if only for the instant rapport it creates. Others are looking for the right 'match' in another category. If you are clear about your whereabouts, you will only attract clients who don't mind, or you may even see the advantages of your location and your way of working.

Time difference, for example, can be convenient in many cases. Imagine an author in Europe hiring an editor in Australia. After the writer finishes his day of work, the editor, on the other side of the world, starts editing. When the writer wakes up the next morning, his prior day's work has already been edited.

A pioneer lifestyle can be a huge advantage, especially for a speaker, consultant, or marketing professional. Dutch captain of industry Herman Wijffels acknowledges this in his recommendation for Esther. "This era needs people who think outside the box, cross borders and create new possibilities. Esther Jacobs is such a person."

NO EXPERIENCE, NO PROBLEM
Depending on the project and the type of work that needs to be done, a client may look at how much experience you have. He will look at your other clients, he will read your recommednations, check your portfolio, and may even check your social media. If you are starting out, it is up to you to build your image as best you can; make sure it is consistent in every way and on every platform.

Some clients believe creativity or talent is more important than experience, and they think that a rookie will be easier on their budget. If you are lucky enough to score another digital nomad as a client, he may be happy to support your endeavors, ignoring lack of experience.

Starting through an agency is a quick way to get clients but it is not well paid. Think about your dream clients and dare to talk to them, offer your services. Try to find your specialization; the tasks you like and that you are really good at.

– Vera Ruttkowski –

DON'T COMPETE ON PRICE

With freelancers in developing countries charging as low as $2 an hour, it is hard to compete in price. So don't even try; you risk not being taken seriously. Serious professionals charge serious rates, based on serious results. Prove that you are worth it and have others back that.

If you are ever in a situation where the other party needs some 'success' in the price negotiation, offer something extra instead of reducing your price. For example, Esther often gets the request for a discounted rate to speak at an event. Instead, she offers to include a number of 'giveaway' books in the original price. Often, this is very much appreciated, and the 'negotiator' (often an event-booker or secretary) can show their boss that they did their job well.

DELIVER QUALITY

Since you won't be competing on price, you can focus on delivering outstanding quality – or, rather, over-delivering. Whether this means injecting your personal style, delivering way before the deadline, or supreme customer service, there are many ways you can make your client happy. If you offer to build somebody's website and you also include some free business advice, it will distinguish you from other website builders.

The book Delivering Happiness (bit.ly/delivering-happiness-zappos), explains Zappo's outstanding customer service and how that makes all other factors nearly irrelevant. Whatever your business is, we are sure you'll be inspired by this story, and find some things you can use in your situation.

FOCUS ON RESULTS INSTEAD OF THE PROCESS

Most of the time, results are all that matter. Many (former) employees and companies, however, are focused on the process. 'If we follow this procedure and allocate a certain amount of hours, then the outcome will automatically be what we want or are used to'.

When asked to do research on a certain topic, you could propose a 'project fee' (instead of an hourly price), for which you promise to deliver a report that meets or exceeds their specific requirements. Result-driven assignments mean that you can organize your own time. If you do it faster than expected, the 'profit' is yours. However, if something takes more time or energy than expected, it's your 'loss'. You will also focus more on results, and get better at predicting how to achieve the best results effectively.

Those who are focused on the process will hire people at hourly rates, require them to log in at certain times, and will try to control the process. They see no other way to influence the outcome. If you are an engineer or consultant visiting a factory, and you see one tiny thing they can change in their machines to increase their production by 3%, what is your added value? Is it the one hour you spent at the factory? At what rate? Maybe they should also pay for your travel expenses? Or is your one remark a result of lifelong training and experience, and should you not look at the process by which it was achieved, but at the result, the added value for the company? How much will they gain or save by your advice? A percentage of that amount may be the right value for your contribution.

OBTAIN KILLER REFERENCES

Better than you saying how good you are (on your website, for example), is when clients say so. Many recommendations and references are about the nice person you are and or how professional your work is. These are 'nice-to-have' references, but the ones you really want are about results. For example: 'After Esther's speech, our sales and marketing department work together like never before' or 'Thanks to X, our new website generated 15% more traffic in the first month'.

Your clients need your help to write these great references. In fact, they probably have no idea how to write them. They will sincerely promise a reference, but they won't have time and won't know what to write. And if they do, it will be something generic and lame. It is best to call them a few weeks after your services to ask how things are going. They will see that as an after-service. With a bit of luck, they will tell you how good your work/service was and what a difference it made to their company. Otherwise, you can just ask for specific results. When they mention something worth having on your website, you can say something like, "I am working on my new website and I would love to use what you just said as a reference. Is that okay? I will put it in writing in an email to you, so you can edit and approve of the text." This will save them time and you will get exactly what you need. Esther wrote a blog with tips on how to get the best references an recommendations: bit.ly/best-ref

Instead of putting a page with references on your website, place one or more references on each page, so they integrate with the rest of the copy and provide the backing of what you say in that section. For example, when Esther lists the various speeches she can give, it is much more powerful if references from previous clients are on the same page.

TAKE ADVANTAGE OF ONLINE PLATFORMS
Try your luck on Fiverr.com; a marketplace for $5 jobs. Test your service, make some easy money, or move on to bigger gigs. Guru.com, Zirtual.com and Upwork.com (formerly Elance) are more serious platforms.

It doesn't hurt to be on LinkedIn either. Make sure you don't use standard phrases, but transfer your authenticity and branding to everything you do. Did you know you can change the standard headline on LinkedIn (drab phrases like 'independent communications professional') to something more fitting? (Esther uses 'No Excuses Lady').

MORE TIPS
A good blog from fellow nomads, with practical tips on how to find clients: bit.ly/freelancer-finding-clients

SHOULD CLIENTS KNOW WHERE YOU ARE?

The fact that you are able to work from anywhere doesn't mean clients will treat you the same when they find out you're halfway around the planet. They either love it and support you, or they turn you down because they prefer to work with someone they can go and drink a coffee with. This is the reality of remote working, but it must be said that clients are becoming more and more open to remote employees, freelancers, and entrepreneurs.

To maximize the chances of scoring a client, some digital nomads prefer not to hint at their location on their website. Others are very open about it. Some actually use their location to their advantage. You will probably have a good sense of what your clients like and don't. And if you're starting out, you may want to experiment with hiding your location, displaying it prominently, or being vague about it.

André is upfront about his location. A map in the sidebar of his website shows where he is, at any given moment. "I don't know how many potential clients I lose, but the ones that do contact me obviously have no qualms about my whereabouts. They will often joke about the weather."

Look at it this way; for work that can be done purely online, it's none of your client's business where you are located. Sure, it can be a fun fact and an icebreaker, but your location should not stand in the way of the quality of your work. In most cases, though, clients won't even notice that you're abroad. Unless, of course, you have applied the Six

Flag Theory (see page 36) and your business is based in a tax haven, which they can see on your invoice.

How about using your location as a Unique Selling Point? Your travels make you into who you are. You probably have fresh ideas and insights, compared to your 'competitors' in the regular 9-5 world. Use this, show it and make your lifestyle part of your offer. Esther's newsletter, for example, is not about her, the projects she has done, or the clients she has landed: "Only two or three times a year, I send out my '5 minutes of inspiration', newsletter with inspiring links and videos I have collected all over the world. Apparently, this is so different, that people are actually constantly asking me when I will send my next newsletter."

INCORPORATING YOUR COMPANY

Even if you are just freelancing, it's recommended to incorporate your business. Without a legal entity, you will likely be categorized as a sole proprietor with unlimited liability - which, depending on the jurisdiction, could mean you are potentially liable personally for any wrongdoing, negligence, or error of the business that affect your customers (or employees, partners, suppliers, others).

If you already lead an international life, or are thinking about traveling for two years or longer, it makes sense to find a company base that is suited to your needs. This may entail setting up shop offshore – possibly in a country you won't ever set foot in.

In the LIVE part of this book, we explained the Six Flag Theory (page 36). This theory proposes spreading your activities, assets and risks over various countries (flags), depending on how welcoming they are, and which advantages they offer. We are the first to admit that this theory is not interesting for –or applicable to– everyone. For example, if you scored 'armchair nomad' in the digital nomad test at the beginning of this book (page 31), you know that you will probably spend most of your time in your home country.

WHERE TO BASE YOUR COMPANY

Whatever you decide to do, clients expect you to send your invoices from a professional company with a fixed base. Even when you live the life of a PT (see page 37), you will need a company structure. The common reporting standard, which recently became effective in 91 countries (or will in 2016 or 2017), will influence your decision on where to base your company.

The common reporting standard basically means that when you open a bank account in one of these countries (basically all the 'interesting' countries, including most off-shore destinations), you have to provide all your personal data, your country of origin and your tax number. At the end of each year all banks in those 91 countries will send your bank balance and any real estate transactions you have made in that year to the tax service in your country of origin. This means that from now on, everything is transparent. Up till now, the secrecy of some countries made them more attractive. On top of that, the tax service in your home country will now know if you have a company or bank account in an offshore area. This can make you look suspicious, not only for possible tax evasion, but might even trigger investigations into terrorism or drugs money.

It seems the solutions that worked well until recently may not be tomorrow's solutions. On the nomad cruise to Brazil Esther had a long talk with a Dutch and German tax advisor. Together they came up with the following 'quick and dirty' advice on where to base your company:

✴ **Your turnover is < €50.000**
It is probably best to stay registered in your own country and keep your company there. Keep it familiar and close. You know the rules and exceptions; you know the various premiums, exemptions etc. If you make sure your travel and other expenses are well documented, there is probably not much profit left to pay tax for.

Of course this all depends on how international your life is. But if you still have ties to your home country (e.g. a house, car, insurance, social life) and you spend the minimum 'required' number of days there, just accept the situation and make the best of it.

★ **Your turnover is between €50.000 and €150.000**
As a European citizen, it might be useful to look into alternative locations for your company within Europe. For example in the UK, Ireland and Estonia it is not too complicated to set up a Ltd (limited liability) company and the corporate taxes are not too bad; they might be lower than in your home country. You will have a European tax number, making it easier to do business in Europe, you will be protected under European law and have rights under the European law (for example to work and move your company within the EU). Keep it as simple as possible in order to avoid excessive expenses, but do get good advice and carefully study the rules and conditions.

★ **Your turnover is > €150.000**
With a six-figure income it can be interesting to look into more complicated (offshore?) structures. However, you will need tax advisors and lawyers in both your home country and the chosen country for your business in order to arrange and research every possible consequence. The expenses you make for this might run into €15.000 or 20.000, so this is not for everybody.

Remember that in most countries, you are considered a resident (or required to become one) if you stay there more than six months a year. Other countries, like Canada, may not look at the time you spend there physically, but rather look at the ties you have to the country.

The country overview on page 64 provides you with an impression of the different rules and tax percentages.

DIGITAL NOMAD PROBLEMS

Esther thought she did well by setting up a company in the British Virgin Islands after the Dutch Chamber of Commerce de-registered her company. She did not live in the Netherlands anymore and spent less than three months a year there. She became a resident in Mallorca, Spain and was enjoying her freedom from administration and tax forms. But the Dutch tax service insisted that she had to pay tax on her world income. Apparently leaving the Netherlands and registering in Spain was not enough 'proof' for them. The Dutch tax authorities maintain that, since she does not pay tax in Spain (she spends too little time there to register with the tax authorities), she has to pay Dutch tax on her world income (including the BVI company). She is fighting this decision, but this requires lots of proof of travel, business etc., which was exactly the administration she was trying to avoid.

Marcus and Feli had a similar experience. They set up a Hong Kong company for their international event business. They stayed registered in Germany and are willing to pay personal income tax. But the German tax authorities now also claim they get an income from their Hong Kong company and want to tax them on that.

It's clear that our (tax) systems are not ready for / adapted to mobile citizens yet. Many authorities see every exaption as a possible 'fraud' case. Until we are consideren legitimate citizens with a different lifestyle and are treated accordingly, we have to find our own way inside the maze, or outside. Let's keep sharing our challenges, problems and (temporary) solutions until we find a more sustainable solution.

HOW TO GET PAID

Once you've established your company, you need to think about how you will get paid for your online work. Below are some of the ways that location-independent entrepreneurs choose to receive their income, whether it is from freelance activities or from selling products. If we specifically look at freelance work, there are online invoicing services that accept many different payment options, thus encouraging clients to pay faster.

SET UP YOUR FINANCIAL INFRASTRUCTURE

Online payments

The obvious choice for fast money transfers is a PayPal.com account. For each transfer, PayPal will charge 3.4%, plus $0.30. You can keep both a euro and a dollar account in PayPal, so you avoid losing money due to conversion rates. For example, Esther keeps the dollars she gets paid for her ebooks in her dollar account in PayPal. When she buys something online in dollars, PayPal automatically deducts that amount from her dollar balance. If the dollar balance is not sufficient, PayPal takes the rest from her euro balance – plus a conversion fee obviously.

Bank account

Whatever you do, don't close the bank account in your home country. It can be a hassle to re-open one once you're overseas (especially if you don't have a registered address anymore). Also, it's more comfortable for clients from your home country to pay into a bank account that's close to home.

Affiliate networks or payment processing companies may only pay out to bank accounts or companies in certain countries. If you need a bank account in the US, in the EU zone, or in the UK, but you're not able to open one from where you are, Payoneer.com is a service that offers a solution. Payoneer gives you virtual US, German, and UK bank accounts, and sends you a MasterCard with which you can withdraw the received payments at any ATM around the world. Setting up your account is free, but withdrawing costs a few dollars/euros/pounds. Where applicable, you pay 2–3.5% more than the mid-market exchange rate.

National payment systems

Some countries have their own payment systems, which allow for fast payments between different banks. In the Netherlands there is iDEAL, India has Net Banking, Germany has a system called Giropay, and the US offers Secure Vault Payments. Customers may feel that their payment is more secure when you offer them this option. Retailers reported significantly improved check-out rates when their clients were given the option to pay through iDEAL in the Netherlands. If you do business in a country or region with such a payment system, you would do well to include it in your payment options.

Credit cards

If you sell digital or tangible products in an online store, you will want to accept credit cards – they are one of the most widely used means of online payment. You can accept credit card payments with your PayPal account, but if you (are expecting to) sell a large volume of products, a merchant account is the logical solution. A merchant account is essentially a middleman that accepts transactions and deposits the money into your bank account. Stripe.com and Authorize.net are two well-known services.

Checks

Especially the US has a strong tradition of payment through personal and certified checks. These are given or mailed to the seller, and include the receiver's details and the amount. They can be cashed at a US post office or bank. When taken to banks outside the US, a minimum amount may be applicable. For example, André's bank in the Netherlands would only cash US checks of $500 and larger.

Automate digital sales

When you sell downloadable products, there are various hosted solutions and WordPress plugins that will accept your client's payment and redirect them to your product. One such service is E-junkie.com. For a flat monthly fee of $5, you can sell as many e-books or courses as you want. Do take into account the cut that PayPal takes for each of the payments you receive.

Gumroad.com is a slick-looking payment processor that targets people who want to sell their music, books, or courses, directly to their customers. Gumroad accepts all major credit cards and pays out to PayPal accounts or US bank accounts. The fee is 5% of your sales price + $0.25.

Sendowl.com is similar to Gumroad as far as the user-interface is concerned, but this service may work out a lot cheaper. You pay a monthly fee of $9.99 for a range of up to 10 downloadable products, which you can sell an unlimited amount of copies of.

For WordPress users, EasyDigitalDownloads.com is a free plugin that accepts PayPal payments by default. It can be expanded with other payment gateways and integrated with your Mailchimp account for a yearly fee.

INVOICING

When sending invoices for the services you render, it is important that you include certain data (like company registration number, VAT number, legal address) on your invoices in order for them to be legally valid in the country you pay tax to. Your accountant or your Chamber of Commerce will be able to tell you what the requirements are. In addition to that, your clients may wish certain codes to be included in the invoices you send them.

Do you ask clients to pay you into your bank account? The IBAN numbering system is slowly rolled out globally; if your bank account has IBAN and SWIFT/BIC codes, make sure to print those on your invoices.

If manually creating and customizing invoices sounds like a lot of work, there are tools that can help you save time and get paid faster. Freshbooks.com is a popular invoicing service that makes charging clients and receiving money from them a breeze. The customization options make the invoices accountant-friendly too, whichever tax authority you pay to. Esther uses Moneybird.nl, an invoicing system for the Netherlands and Germany. She had a custom integration with her WooCommerce web shop built, so everything connects and syncs perfectly.

VAT

In most countries, you are required to charge a sales tax on the services or products you sell. This Value Added Tax (VAT) is called MwSt in Germany, IVA in Spain, TVA in France, BTW in the Netherlands and מיסים עקירים in Hebrew. Depending on where you incorporate, your company will get a VAT number, which needs to be printed on your invoices. If your client is a company, you will be required to print his VAT number on the invoice as well.

The VAT system works well when companies, clients, and products, have clear locations and origins. But what if Esther is in Brazil while her BVI company sells a Skype coaching session to a German client, who happens to be in Thailand when the sale or session takes place? Which country's VAT needs to be applied then? They are still trying to figure that out. In the meantime, you officially have to use the VAT of the country where your client is based. Systems like PayPal automatically use the country of the buyers bank account as a base. In Esther's case this means 21% BTW (Dutch) VAT will be automatically added by PayPal. Very annoying when your purchase has nothing to do with the country your bank account is in…

Offshore companies that don't need to pay any tax don't need a VAT number. Officially, you have to get a VAT registration in each country you do business with (meaning in each country you have clients). A way around this (for services or products delivered outside of the EU to EU businesses) is to create invoices without VAT, stating that the VAT is deferred. This means, the client needs to register the VAT over their purchase, which they can then deduct again. It makes no difference financially to anybody; but it saves you the hassle of registering and having to file tax reports in each country.

In summary, VAT, or your local equivalent, is easy to understand and apply when your company and your clients are located in the same country. However, as soon as you start delivering services and billing clients outside your company's country, things may get complicated. Digital nomads are often in the 'grey zone', so keep an eye on developments and ask expert advice.

WORK SMART, NOT HARD

We became digital nomads to enjoy more freedom and live life more fully, not necessarily to relocate our over-crowded workdays to a sunnier location. When Esther visited the legendary coworking spot Hubud in Ubud, Bali, she was puzzled to see hundreds of digital nomads typing away at their laptops in a space apparently too small to hold them all. There was no air conditioning, only some fans; it was very hot and humid. Everybody kept staring at their screens and working like there was no tomorrow. Sure, there was a view of the rice fields out of one of the windows, but nobody seemed to notice. Across the road was an open air cafe with good Wi-Fi, with beautiful views (and sounds!) of the rice fields, and a nice, cool breeze. "Why weren't they working there? Why were they all working so hard, anyway?" she wondered.

In order to be successful online, you will need to make sacrifices. You won't be able to see all the sights if you also want to make some money. Sometimes, you will have to let go of a project you are madly in love with, because doesn't bring you the desired income fast enough. There will be moments when you'll be brimming with good ideas, but lack the discipline and patience to focus on just one project. It will be hard work, which we don't mind, as long as we're working on the right projects, and doing it in a smart and productive way.

Doing something unimportant very well, doesn't make it important. The fact that something is taking a lot of time, doesn't make it important.
– Timothy Ferriss, author, (timothyferriss.com) –

Many digital nomads think that outsourcing is the solution to productivity challenges. This can definitely be very helpful, but you need to get organized first before you can outsource successfully.

BEFORE HIRING A VA - BY PATTY GOLSTEIJN

I see it all the time: self-employed professionals doing things in the wrong order. You feel overwhelmed with the amount of work and you decide you should get a virtual assistant. Great! But that's actually the last step to take.

Hiring a VA when you 'don't have your shit together' means you're getting nowhere faster. It won't save you any time or energy. It's just more work.

It takes time and effort to onboard a VA and build a relationship. If you want to get the most from collaborating with a VA, there are a few other steps to take first.

✦ Eliminate
Your biggest problem is you've taken on too much. First, get rid of everything that doesn't need to be done at all. Projects that you don't like, partnerships that aren't working and products that don't feel right.

✦ Simplify
Create a workflow for all recurring processes, such as an ecourse, webinar or 1-on-1 coaching. Write down every single detail. When it's all in your head, it's harder to connect the dots. Get it in front of you. You'll see roadblocks you can tackle, surplus work you're doing and duplicate steps to get rid of.

✦ Automate
There are so many wonderful tools out there. You're probably doing a lot of work that can be done by other services. Whenever you have to do something twice, google it. Want to bet someone else got there before you and created an app for it? Or ask someone who knows online tools.

✳ Outsource

Yep, now you see why this is the last step. If you've done the first three steps correctly, there is not much left to outsource. Which is a good thing, because I've just saved you money and time in the long run.

Patty is an expert in minimizing. More insights and advice? Go to:

 pattygolsteijn.com

In this chapter, we will help you reduce the amount of work, and look into the skills, tools, attitude and bag of tricks of a location-independent worker. These can make a huge difference in the way you organize your work, and structure your day.

We do have to print a small disclaimer here. In the fast-paced internet age, anything over a year is old, and one tool seems to spur demand for the next. Developers never run out of ideas and the world never runs out of developers, resulting in an avalanche of apps, software, websites and tools. The list in this book may already be outdated by the time it is printed, so once you hit the road, you will undoubtedly come across many new tools. One way to stay updated is to share the latest tools and tricks in one of the Digital Nomad groups on Facebook (page 265).

MINIMIZE THE AMOUNT OF WORK

Most digital nomads have unlocked the secret to a happy life – freedom. The internet is their 'great enabler', and although they may be on a mission to change the world through their product or service, they never lose sight of what's important in life. That's why they jump at the chance to increase their efficiency. The four steps Patty Golsteijn mentioned for hiring a VA can be perfectly adapted for minimizing your workload.

1) ELIMINATE

Stop doing things that are not essential. Look at your goals and objectives; they may be income motivated or include 'having fun' or 'only working with people you like'. Then scan which projects and tasks contribute to your life goal and which are just distractions. If in doubt, stop doing that activity. That way, you'll only spend your time and energy on projects and activities that make you happy, one way or another.

You can apply the 80-20 rule to almost anything. Probably 80% of your income comes from 20% of your clients. If there are annoying clients among the other 80%, 'fire' them! Yes, you can fire clients as well. Good is good enough. Focus on work that gets you 80% of results with 20% of the effort. If you desire to get that last 20% to obtain perfection, it will probably cost you 80% more time.

2) SIMPLIFY

Get organized. Analyze your processes. Anything recurring can be done better, faster, smarter, easier; only after you carefully identify each step of the process. Make sure another person can exactly replicate what you are doing by reading your instructions. This is essential to the next steps: automating and outsourcing.

Esther found out that many emails and requests she gets involve the same topics and questions. She put these Frequently Asked Questions (FAQ's) and their answers on her website. Now, all she has to do when people ask her for advice about writing their book, becoming a professional speaker, charity projects, etc., is direct them to her website. The added advantage is that her website now provides so much content that it generates more traffic.

3) AUTOMATE

It is a waste of time to repeat things that a tool can do faster or take care of altogether. Below are programs and apps that help us save time at work. You'll find many smart tips and apps on sites like Lifehacker.com. These are our favorites:

Write faster

We all have words, url's and phrases, we regularly type. By using a tool like TextExpander (bit.ly/get-text-expander), you accelerate your typing through keyboard shortcuts that you configure. For example, you could set the key combination 'tthank', to expand into 'Thank you for your email.' Esther also uses Textexpander to 'remember' her various phone numbers, frequently used addresses, bank accounts, and URLs. The software keeps its own statistics, and recently announced that she had already saved 10(!) hours of typing.

If you are a blogger or a copywriter and produce a lot of content, why not let your computer do the typing? Speech recognition software such as Dragon NaturallySpeaking (nuance.com/dragon) lets you boost your 'typing' speed to around 150 words per minute. A cheaper workaround is using the dictation option on your iPhone.

Remember your passwords

How many sites and apps do we need login details for? They easily run into the hundreds. If you don't want to use the same password for all websites – and we know you don't – you will have to memorize an awful lot of passwords. Storing them in a note or other document makes you vulnerable to hackers. By keeping them in a secure online vault, you'll never have to worry about this again. LastPass.com and 1Password (agilebits.com/onepassword) both do a good job of detecting when you need to type a username/password combination and will offer to memorize these for you. Esther also keeps her credit card details, PIN codes, software licenses, passport, drivers license, and other sensitive information in 1Password. When you store the master file on Dropbox, instead of locally on your computer, you can access the same data from your phone or tablet, plus you'll have a backup in the cloud.

Manage your social media accounts

If you have a blog or manage an online business, keeping your audience engaged will be one of your worries. Posting photos, quotes, info graphics, polls, links, and thoughts on your social media accounts is a lot easier when you can keep everything within one dashboard. Hootsuite.com and Buffer.com help you plan and queue your tweets and status updates. Indispensable for community managers. However, keep in mind that direct (Facebook) posts get a higher ranking than posts through platforms like Hootsuite or Buffer.

If This Then That

IFTTT.com is a brilliant site, which does exactly what its name indicates. You can link various websites and applications to create your own 'recipes'. For example, "If the Weather Channel predicts good surfing weather, send me a text message". Or "If anybody tags a picture of me on Facebook, save it in my Photo app". Google 'ifttt recipes' to find out the original and useful recipes people around the world are inventing.

Your admin on the go

If the country where your company is registered requires you to keep an administration, look into Evernote. With the app Scannable (bit.ly/evernote-scannable) on your phone, you can take pictures of every receipt, name or tag it, and store it in your bookkeeping folder, which you can share with your assistant or accountant. Shoeboxed.com is an online service that makes scanning and organizing your receipts, business cards, and expense overviews, easy. ("Turn receipts into data"). As they charge per receipt, this is a good idea for the larger expenses, not the tiny daily ones.

4) OUTSOURCE

Anybody can hire a virtual assistant or freelancer, even if you are a freelancer yourself. Did you know you can outsource any task that you find boring or difficult? The best tasks to outsource are:

* easy to explain
* repetitive
* and can be done online.

Start with small jobs, experiment with different people, tasks, and platforms. You need to learn to work like this step by step for it to be effective.

Need to get a logo made, have a blog article written, or get some online research done? For these and thousands of other digital jobs, Fiverr.com is the ideal marketplace. Here, you can order 'gigs' from as low as $5. You often get what you pay for, but even just browsing this website is a lot of fun.

If you are looking for more serious help, Guru.com, Zirtual.com, and Upwork.com (formerly Elance and Odesk.com), are good marketplaces to look for freelancers. Post a job and see what proposals you get, or select freelancers by expertise and rating, and invite them to bid on your project.

By the way, did you know that Upwork runs a fun digital nomad blog? (bit.ly/live-life-free)

Esther has been working with various VAs from Asia, Eastern Europe and the US, and shares her tips:

- ★ I prefer to work with a person instead of a company; extra levels mean higher costs, and more risk of miscommunication.

- ★ VAs come and go. You might work with somebody for several years and suddenly they disappear or have other priorities and you need to find a new VA.

- ★ I pay about $10 per hour, sometimes a bit more for specialized tasks (like design).

- ★ In some countries saying 'yes' doesn't mean they actually understand, sometimes they just say what they think you want to hear. I started working with somebody from India, but found the language/cultural barrier too difficult. The Philippines was a bit better, but right now I have several assistants from Eastern Europe and am very happy with their work.

- ★ In the selection process, review references and have various VA's perform the same task to find out who works best, who has creative ideas, asks intelligent questions, and who respects deadlines.

- ★ Trust your guts. Sometimes you really want/need an assistant, but the person you found just doesn't feel right. Don't invest in a person/relationship when you have doubts; continue until you find a perfect fit.

- ★ Don't expect one person to be able to do everything. Some VA's are very good at one line of work and others are great at other tasks. Always ask their 'specialty' and what makes them happy. Working with happy assistants makes your own life a lot happier as well!

- ★ I have a Dutch assistant for typical Dutch things, such as archiving and tagging my media clippings and maintaining my Dutch website. An English-speaking assistant, who is also a designer, does my (English) website work and some design/photo editing tasks.

- ★ After a few projects, I tend to share my login details. Some other entrepreneurs are very reluctant about this. But how can you work with somebody if you can't trust them?

FOCUS AND PRODUCTIVITY

Traveling from place to place means that you don't have a fixed workplace. This may be exactly what you wanted back in the old office days, but you must be prepared for some productivity challenges.

One of the reasons for getting less done may be the lack of a suitable workplace. Whether it's the heat in a tropical country, a slow connection at the local library, or the lack of a desk in your room, we all have wants and needs that, until they are met, prevent us from working flat out. So find out what factors are important to you for optimal productivity (temperature? good chairs? silence? time of day?) and make sure these conditions are met when you really want to get some work done.

Another distraction is an obvious one: you're in a new place that you're excited to explore. You simply don't want to spend all day working like you were used to back home. You've declared your freedom and now you want to enjoy it.

And of course, wherever you are, social media can be huge distractions. 'Zapping' through your Facebook timeline all day is probably not why you moved your life to this exotic location. If you can't contain yourself, you might consider what digital nomad Maneesh Sethi did. He hired a girl to slap him in the face every time he checked Facebook. 😊

Generally speaking, the more you move about, the less time/energy you have for quality work. Sometimes, it just makes more sense to spend a while in one spot, so you can focus. Working on a big project, facing a deadline, or trying to get your first online business off the ground, are some of the situations that don't combine well with travel. While finishing this book, for example, Esther was travelling in Brazil. She got so frustrated with the small amount of work she could get done, that she rented an air conditioned hotel room with a proper desk and stayed there for two weeks until the book was finished. Find suitable workplaces to suit your activities. For example, for brainstorming sessions, you may want to go to a particular cafe, while for Skype calls with clients, you may prefer a shared office space with reliable Wi-Fi. Staying longer in one spot has the added advantage of finding the cheapest options for living, working, and playing there.

Inspired by books like The Four Hour Workweek and Gettings Things Done, some online entrepreneurs prioritize and carry out their work in a very structured way. They install browser plugins to block time-killers, like Facebook, online newspapers and YouTube, and they work in 25-minute pomodoros, after which they take a 5-minute rest. Ideally, email is only checked and answered twice a day. Find out what works best for you.

Because personal productivity and motivation are the most impor-tant and interesting skills for digital nomads, Esther teamed up with two other location independent entrepreneurs and created an e-course on the topic: GetShitDoneCourse.com

EMAIL EFFICIENCY

Email is time-consuming and can be mind-numbing. Constantly reacting to impulses from the outside world distracts you from your real work and/or creativity. Therefore, try to limit yourself to fixed times and stick to strict rules.

* Don't check your email first thing in the morning. This will give you the chance to get some real work done (pro-active) before you go into the re-active mode.
* It is no longer necessary to make a separate folder for each pro-ject or client. With good search functions nowadays, you can always search by name or topic.
* It is more logical to archive your emails in folders labeled with actions (to do, reading, waiting for, payments to be made, etc.). This way you can work on batches of mails that require the same

sort of action, which is more efficient. The rest goes into your main archive, which contains everything you don't specifically need right now.

- ✸ Your inbox is not a to-do list. Archive to-dos in 'actions' folders.
- ✸ Check your inbox only 1, 2 or 3 times a day, at fixed times. Can something be dealt with in two minutes? Then do it immediately. Otherwise, move the mail to your action folder, so your mailbox will remain empty. In this way, you can work within your action files without being disturbed by new mail.
- ✸ Use clear subject lines (which action is required from whom) for your emails, and train others to do the same.

TOOLS WE LOVE

Digital nomads love tools. No wonder, since it is these very tools that allow them to work from anywhere. From work-specific tools, via travel-themed apps, to websites; we've collected the most popular tools for the digital nomad crowd to help you work smarter.

Create and edit documents

Have you just sent your client a document in Apple Pages, only to find out that he needs an MS Word version? Or have you edited a spreadsheet in OpenOffice Calc and does exporting it to an MS Excel file go completely wrong? Google Docs is the platform-independent solution that allows you to edit documents, spreadsheets and presentations from any internet-enabled device.

Google Docs is accessible from any internet browser. You decide who to share the documents with: just enter an email address to give view, comment, or edit rights to a specific person, or copy the URL to allow anyone access who has the link. Multiple persons can work in a document at the same time, and you can see (and approve or decline) who edited what. You won't have to worry about your computer crashing, either. Google documents are constantly auto-saved.

Blogging software

If you don't have a website yet, chances are you will go with the world's preferred blogging platform, WordPress. One of the reasons for its success is the fact that it is open-source software. Developers are constantly improving the software, and offer free and paid plugins. There are thousands of templates –called themes– for sale to help you create the desired look and feel for your website.

WordPress is a number one favorite with travel bloggers, but can also be used for e-commerce sites, thanks to plugins like WooCommerce webshop. The many tutorials on Youtube can teach you how to set up your own site and web shop. If you need help, Marika Porrey (web-sidekick.com) offers Skype teaching and assistance with the more technical parts.

Update your to-do list

As a nomad, one of your luxury problems is having to resist a lot of temptations: snorkeling tours, volcano climbs, horse rides, sundowners, and surf sessions. In the midst of these distractions, solutions like Trello.com and Wunderlist.com help you prioritize. They both have a web app for the easy compilation of to-do lists, while their phone and tablet apps allow you to add tasks or tick them off on the go.

Use short links

Bitly.com allows you to shorten long or complicated links (for example, affiliate links, deeplinks into your website, etc.), and even customize them. It also keeps track of statistics (clicks, opens, referrals, etc.). Use them in your ebooks, newsletters, and more, and get strategic feedback and information.

Test your Wi-Fi speed

Whether you're moving into a long-term rental or you're checking out the local cafes, a Wi-Fi speed test will tell you which places to avoid and which to come back to. There are numerous apps and websites that will do the trick, but Speedtest.net seems the obvious choice.

When renting an airbnb apartment, ask the host to send you a screenshot of the speedtest for a realistic idea of the internet speed in the apartment.

Protect your eyes

The blue light of computer, tablet, and smartphone screens affects our sleep cycle, keeping us up late. The app F.lux (justgetflux.com) runs in the background and adjusts colors in a way that reduces the stimulating effects of blue light. If you're an early riser, for example, you will notice your screen has a reddish glow to it, which supposedly helps your body to wake up.

Keep a journal

Many bloggers like to start the day by typing 750 or 1000 words into a Google Doc or journaling software. This helps them to get in the writing flow, and may or may not result in useful content for upcoming posts. Journaling can help you gain clarity; it is amazing how much clearer things become when you expose them in writing. Also, it can help you set goals and track progress. DayOneApp.com is a popular diary app for Apple users, while TheJournal.ie is suitable to all platforms.

Store and share files

Sure, Google Docs gives you a few gigabytes of space, but there are more interesting services out there. Dropbox.com, for example, integrates seamlessly with your local folder structure. It allows you to easily upload large files to the 'cloud' and share it with whomever you like. Mega (mega.co.nz) is relatively new. Though uploading and downloading is slower, and can only be done through a browser window, it offers 50 GB of storage space.

Evernote.com is also a great option. The web app and the mobile app boast an incredible search engine, which recognizes text in your documents, and even in pictures. Do a Google search to find creative ways in which writers, project managers, etc. use Evernote for their projects.

Collaborate

Part-up.com is a new marketplace for teamwork. It helps you get temporary virtual teams together. Post your dream or project, and people from all over the world can sign up for your temporary team. You are free to choose what you work on and who you work with. Together, you decide on the activities and what each will contribute. You build your profile and show the world what you're good at. You can also get your own part-up tribe to start working together with your local community, network, or organization.

Slack

Slack.com is a chat platform that was built by the founder of Flickr. It helps teams to eliminate emails and has a powerful search function. Thanks to its user friendliness and availability on all kinds of platforms, Slack is gaining popularity with teams who want to keep all their internal communication in one handy dashboard.

Keep track of time zones

What's the current time in New York, Singapore or Auckland? There is no need to type this question into Google every time you're at a new destination. EveryTimeZone.com shows you what the time is right now in metropoles around the world. If you are working with a distributed team or clients all over the world, then you can use Timezone.io to keep track of local times.

COWORKING OFFICES

Want to meet other digital nomads? Need to focus in a productive environment? Looking for inspiration? Whatever you are looking for in a workplace, you'll probably find it in a coworking space. They've only been around for about ten years, but it looks like they're here to stay.

In 2005, software engineer Brad Neuberg created a collective work space that was only accessible two days a week. The owners of the space, friends of his, kindly asked him to leave no permanent additions, since they were running a business on the remaining week-days. This meant that Neuberg had to set up and break down his folding tables each of the days he had access to the space.

Naïvely, Neuberg thought that a Craigslist ad would be enough to bring in a steady stream of what he called 'coworkers'. In fact, nobody came for the first month. Only when Neuberg went out to the coffee shops to talk to laptop workers did the idea catch on. He went on to open a 'co living' space, the Hat Factory, which hosted up to 10 workers per day. Neuberg was also a founding member of one of San Francisco's most famous coworking offices: Citizen Space.

Unwittingly, Neuberg had started a movement that spread like a wildfire over the San Francisco area, then the USA, and ultimately the rest of the world. Nowadays, there are few cities without coworking spaces.

Reasons to work in a coworking office:

* Enjoy fast internet

  While a domestic internet connection is usually reliable, cafes and libraries can't guarantee a fast or stable network. And when it's time for that all-or-nothing Skype call, you want to make sure you can count on your Wi-Fi . Generally, a coworking space has a fast, business-grade internet connection. Even at full occupancy, with heads all around you bopping to streaming music, you will be able to hold a videoconference or webinar.

★ Beat the boredom

Many location-independent workers decide to work from home. And by 'home', we also mean a hotel room or any other temporary accommodation. Working from the same home office can get rather boring, though. Coworking offices allow you to sit at a shared table, out in a courtyard or on a rooftop terrace, or even an on-site cafe.

★ Escape the chaos

Working at home need not be boring. On the contrary, it can be very stressful if you have small children, or when you have friends or family stay over. When you're working toward a tight deadline, or simply need a quiet and professional workspace, a coworking office is ideal.

★ Save money on lattes

Location-independent workers who do go out to cafes can easily rack up hundreds of dollars or euros a month in food and drink expenses. Most coworking spaces allow you to join for less than that amount, and offer all-you-can-drink coffee.

★ Meet like-minded workers

If you stick to your home office or local cafes, it is easy to think there are few location-independent workers like you. You may feel isolated and will start to miss the social interaction that prevents office workers from going insane. In a coworking space, you will meet like-minded workers, making you realize the movement is growing.

★ New business opportunities

Surrounding yourself with other location-independent professionals means you have easy access to tax advisers, designers, developers, or marketing experts, to name just a few examples. This also works the other way around; your next client may be at that coworking space. Many startups were born in coworking offices, where online entrepreneurs and freelancers decided to combine their unique skills to offer a new product or service.

★ Receive clients in a professional environment
When you have an important meeting with a client, the meeting room in a coworking space is the perfect place to talk business. This same room can be utilized (usually at no extra cost) if you plan to organize a seminar or workshop.

Have we forgotten to mention some of the advantages of coworking spaces? Most likely. However, the point is that coworking spaces are the ideal environments for digital nomads. With a travel schedule and a lifestyle that can be hectic, the last thing you want to do is leave your business success to chance. It's no wonder that one of the first things nomads do, when moving to their next destination, is look up the local coworking offices and, if possible, reserve a desk or work space ahead of their arrival. Some of the spaces are free, others offer day passes or monthly memberships. You can also travel between spaces internationally, using the Coworking Visa (bit.ly/cowork-visa): a program that allows active members to use another participating space in a different city, free of charge.

Various websites attempt to provide overviews of coworking spaces around the world. desksurfing.net lists almost 700 locations. There's also a coworking wiki with a coworking space directory (bit.ly/coworking-wiki): please help to improve these lists.

There are other great places to work and meet other nomads. In the next section of this book, PLAY, you can read about workations, coliving concepts, digital nomad cruises, and many more ways to combine living, working and playing, location-independently.

PLAY

Play is the highest form of research.

Albert Einstein

STEP OUT OF YOUR COMFORT ZONE

Many people know what they want, and also how to achieve it. What keeps them from realizing their dream is that they have trouble stepping out of their comfort zone. Becoming a digital nomad is doing exactly that. You know the life you have (even if you don't like it any more), but you don't know what's waiting for you when you leave everything behind and step into this new life. Therefore, you'll probably make excuses that this is not the right time, there are other priorities, or you need more money, experience, or other resources. Don't fall for it! The external circumstances will never be perfect. Take what you have and make the best of it. Take the plunge!

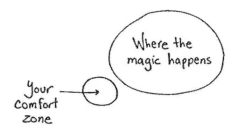

This section of the book will give you more insight into what your life could look like. Ideas of what you could do, places you could go. You will need this leverage to overcome the hurdles you will inevitably encounter. So dive into it; visualize your dream live, feel the sun on your skin, the adrenaline in your body and the smile on your face.

Sometimes you need a little nudge to get started. Whatever you do: don't burn bridges; take small steps, one at the time.
Esther had been thinking for years about becoming a full-blown digital nomad, deregistering from The Netherlands, and setting up an international identity. Even though her life was already pretty international, she remained reluctant to make the official step. She did not know how the Dutch tax authorities would react, how she would arrange her insurance, etc. She was pretty comfortable with the way things were. When she got 'fired' from her own country for traveling too much, at first it seemed like her world fell apart. But then, step-

by-step, she found solutions to every problem and slowly started to see the project as a challenge. "Just because I made the first step, and then the second, and the third, at some point I was in the middle of it and I became confident that I would also be able to take the next steps."

If you want to become a freelancer or an online entrepreneur, don't immediately give up your current job. Start with the first steps in your spare time: a business plan, website, networking, first projects or clients. As soon as it catches on, you can consider cutting one workday a week and spending that extra day on your own business. When you start generating sufficient income and feel confident enough, you can slowly transition to being self-employed. Should you choose to begin your business directly, you could take on freelance assignments in order to generate some temporary income.
If you want to become a digital nomad, first go on a 'workation' (more info on page 269) to meet like-minded people and to experiment with working abroad. Or you could do a house-swap for some months before burning all your bridges.

Don't wait for the right moment
Everything is a choice; even refraining from choosing – be aware of this. Waiting until the kids are older, until work is less busy, until you have saved enough money, until you or your partner retires, until you no longer have to take care of your parents, until you have found the right partner, and so on, realize that the perfect moment, when all circumstances are ideal, will never come. There will always be some reason or excuse for why you should not yet do what you actually want to do deep down in your heart.

If you wait for this moment, your dream will never come true. Everyone who has pursued their dreams says that, at a given moment, they simply made the first step, and the rest just followed. Most problems can be overcome along the way.

Hilda and Bas from the Netherlands sailed with their small kids to and through the Caribbean. At first the project seemed too big and bold and was doomed to stay a dream. But when they made a hypothetical plan, it suddenly seemed realistic and they decided to just do it.

"For a while, we'd had a vague wish to spend some time away, in fair weather, on the water. Friends of ours had spent a year sailing, and we thoroughly enjoyed their stories. At the same time, it was out of the question that we would ever give up our interesting jobs and cozy existence in the Netherlands. Hilda felt that she first had to achieve something career-wise before she would deserve such a trip. Thinking of it in this way, the plans never became tangible. Postponing would turn into abandonment.

Then, we decided to turn it into a hypothetical project, with lists of wishes and requirements, and an estimated budget. Hypothetically, we discussed, "Say we were to go. What would we do and how would we go about it?" If you chop such a project into pieces and articulate it into concrete points of action, it actually becomes quite coherent. Then we came to the realization - we'll just do it, and soon! It felt like a kind of momentum that we needed to gain. Everything fell into place.

We both took navigation classes and we followed a medical course at Rotterdam's famous harbor medical center. We got in touch with a friendly doctor who would assist us via radio during our trip, if needed. We learned the most essential things for when you're at sea for a few weeks. For example, stitching wounds (which we practiced on a chicken leg). Before we knew it, the day of departure had come. It was quite emotional to say goodbye to family and friends for a whole year. It was, therefore, extra special when they visited us during our trip. These shared vacations were an enormous bonus. How often do you get to travel with your parents or good friends? During our trip, we got an idea to start our own business: tapasclub. nl. We now sell authentic tapas to wholesalers, caterers and cafes in Northern Europe, and we still travel regularly to Spain." 🙂

YOUR BUCKET LIST

Now you are free to go wherever you want and to do what you always wanted to do. Have you already made a list of 'things to do before I die'? What's on your so-called bucket list? Are you going to learn something new? Explore new destinations? Help others? The possibilities are endless. In this section we will give you some ideas.

HOBBY OR ACTIVITY

What is your hobby? What did you want to do when you were younger? Maybe you dreamed of becoming a professional tennis player, or always loved dancing. Now that you're location-independent and possibly even time-independent (we're referring to passive income), you have the opportunity to spend more time on your hobby. So, why not find the best place in the world to develop your skill? It's not only a great way to develop yourself, but also a fantastic excuse to get to know a country, city or culture. There are so many possibilities:

- ✴ Tango dancing in Buenos Aires, Argentina
- ✴ Spanish and/or salsa in Cuba
- ✴ Learn to sail -and perhaps establish a business- in the British Virgin Islands (BVI)
- ✴ A massage course in Thailand
- ✴ Yoga in Indonesia. You could also buy furniture and other items to sell elsewhere in the world...
- ✴ Cooking in Italy

- Acting in Hollywood
- Martial arts in Japan
- Kite surfing and mountain biking and a wine course and... in South Africa
- Photography in New York
- Learn Catalan in Barcelona (This might seem like a 'useless' language, until you notice how happy the locals are when you try to speak their language.)
- Design in London
- 'Something technical' in Silicon Valley
- A diving course in the Philippines
- Surfing in Hawaii

Did you know there's a website where you can track your own goals, find inspiration and track other people's progress? bucketlist.org

In my early twenties, I made a bucket list with the countries I wanted to visit and things I wanted to experience. Instead of waiting until I had enough money/time/security, I just went ahead and started 'ticking' things off my list. Within a year, I managed to complete my personal top 10. I walked the famous Inca trail in Peru to visit the mystical sacred ruins of Machu Picchu. I learned to speak Portuguese while traveling in Brazil; I lived on a tropical island and swam with wild dolphins. I piloted a small plane, and even a helicopter. I parachute jumped out of a plane, with a minute-long free-fall. I did not think about my career or pension; rather, I just opened up to what came my way. Living in the moment and fulfilling my dreams gave me so much energy!

This attitude enabled me to follow my instincts, even though rationally it might not seem all too logical. This lifestyle created so many learning opportunities. I got to know myself really well and found inspiration all over the world. As a speaker, and in my books and workshops, I now share all these experiences with others.

– Esther Jacobs –

THEME

Instead of a location or activity, you can also plan your journey around a certain theme.

* Culture. Visit all former colonies of your country, or all countries where your language is spoken. It will probably also be easier to find temporary work there.
* Charity. Help others. Work as a volunteer (more on page 253). Teach English in children's homes, etc. Blog about your experiences. Maybe your friends would want to sponsor you and support some of the projects you encounter on the road.
* Beaches. Discover the most beautiful beaches in the world. This 'traveler's choice' top 25 TripAdvisor could be a guideline: bit.ly/25-beaches
* Nightlife. Visit the coolest bars, concerts and parties, such as the full moon party in Koh Phangan, Thailand, or the North Sea Jazz Festival in Curaçao, etc.
* Peace and solitude. How about visiting the 33 most desolate places in the world? bit.ly/33-abandoned
* Photography. Capture the essence of these bizarre places, or discover new locations. bit.ly/27-surreal
* Cities. If you like the buzz of cities, Check Conde Nast Travelers' list of 30 popular cities: bit.ly/30bestcities
* Friends and family. Visit all the people you know and/or make new friends through Facebook, Couchsurfing, etc. Dave Gorman visited people who shared his first name and surname... Amazon still has copies of the 2002 book: bit.ly/davegorman
* Make a tour of the most special places to stay on Airbnb. How about an igloo or a castle?
* Anthropology. Discover and experience cross-cultural diversity. The Lewis model might be a good guideline: bit.ly/lewis-model
* Food. Eat yourself through Italy, like Julia Roberts did in Eat, Pray, Love. Or follow your own palate and make your journey about local food. Meet real people who usually gather in small

markets. Lawyer Jodi Ettenberg did just that, and eventually created a business with food blogs, a travel food book, and food walks in Asia. Her blog: legalnomads.com

What is your theme? Is there something that is really characteristic for you? Something you've always wanted to explore or study? Something you've dreamed about since you were a child? This is your chance to make that the central focus of your life and/or travels.

I love my life –even though sometimes it's very tough and stressful– and would rather jump off a cliff than going to back to work for someone else.

Some of the most memorable things that have happened along my journey:
- ★ *Watching the most incredible and colored sunrise above the ocean in Thailand at 6 am*
- ★ *Backpacking on my snowboard across the Switzerland / Italy border on the alps*
- ★ *Kayaking along the Mekong river in Cambodia to check out pink dolphins*
- ★ *Surfing in Peru with sea lions popping out of the water*
- ★ *Training at 4000 meters of altitude in Cusco, Peru*
- ★ *Holding and feeding a sloth in the Amazon jungle, in Peru*
- ★ *Swimming with sharks, giant sea turtles, sea lions in the Galapagos islands, Ecuador*
- ★ *Whale watching from a boat - but constantly falling asleep because I had taken nausea pills… in Ecuador*
- ★ *Farming fresh salt from the sea and cliff jumping in Malta*
- ★ *Accidentally eating a cake that contained drugs, thinking I was just enjoying a really good chocolate cake in Laos. In fact, it was on the most horrible experiences I've ever had, but I still think it's pretty epic!*

– Martina Russo –

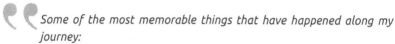

A CHALLENGE

If you like challenges, why don't you invent one to spice up your travels? Apart from the kick you will get from stepping out of your comfort zone, you will most probably learn something new, inspire others, maybe get some media attention, and possibly even generate some business, out of your 'crazy idea'.

Some examples of personal challenges:

⭐ The 100 person project. In 2011, Shenee Howard was broke, confused, and couldn't get a client, despite her expensive education. She decided she needed a change, but didn't know where to start. So she started talking. To 100 people. About anything. Sometimes, she could help them by brainstorming about their business. Four months later, she sold out her first e-course, helping people with the questions she got asked most often. Shenee now runs a successful business in 'brand chemistry'. Watch her story on bit.ly/shenee-howard. She even offers your own '100 people project' to "help you get clarity, build your community and figure out your next steps." More info on bit.ly/100-people-project.

⭐ Embracing rejection; another 100 day project. Jia Jiang was so devastated when investors rejected the proposal he had been working on so hard in his trial year as an entrepreneur, he decided to face rejection head on. He started to make ridiculous requests (like asking police officers if he could ride in their car, and random strangers if he could play soccer in their backyard), expecting to be turned down each time. To his surprise, he started getting more and more 'yesses'. His story is hilarious and contagious. It led to speeches, a book, and he now runs his own business. Watch how 'the donuts' were a life-changing experience on bit.ly/100-rejection.

⭐ Share your way home. Rob Greenfield invited others to 'share his way home', from Panama back to the USA. Not only did he not carry any money; he also left his phone back home. The documentary of his trip was entirely filmed by the people he met on the road. robgreenfield.tv/share-my-way-home

- 30-days-helping-a-friend. Entrepreneur Tal Gur (page 157) has a pretty long and very specific life-goal list (bit.ly/100-life-goals). One of those goals is, for 30-days straight, to help at least one friend in need. When Tal was invited to become an advisor in an entrepreneur startup program, he decided that it was time to face the helping-a-friend challenge. He posted on Facebook, "Get one hour of my time and heart for free to support you in whatever way you need." People signed up and they did the meetings live, via Skype or phone. Tal's describes his most profound takeaways; "I got into the mindset of 'giving first' and doing so without expecting anything in return. This attitude opened doors for me in so many ways. I met people who I never would have met otherwise. I gained invaluable insights which I never would have found otherwise, and perhaps more importantly, I connected more deeply with myself, who I want to be, and what I'm here to do." Read his blog for more details: talgur.me/giving-first
- Let the readers of your blog determine your life. Colin Wright moves to another country every four months, each location decided by his followers. bit.ly/colin-wright
- Living without money. Retired Heidemarie Schwermer travels around without possessions or money, trying to make others aware of how attached we have become to material things: bit.ly/Heidemarie
- Drunken bet. What do you do when you wake up hung-over, realizing you've made the silliest bet? Comedian Tony Hawks found out he had been challenged to travel round Ireland with a fridge. His pride and £100 were at stake, so there was no way Tony could refuse. Check out the travel book on Amazon: bit.ly/roundireland

Half Spanish, half Dutch Sylvia Lorente van Bergen Henegouwen (1976) is as European as they get. She studied in France, lives in Germany, and has helped develop over 400 mobile apps. She took a sabbatical from her job as a startup mentor to travel to 12 world cities in 12 months.

When I tried to buy a flat in Barcelona and someone else offered more money, I actually got a feeling of relief. In my work we had just experienced several years of intense growth. We were in the process of selling the company and were in the final months of the earn out which made it very intense. All of that made it good time for thinking of a next step. And I started to doubt if I should stay in Barcelona – it was a great city, but was it great professionally? Was my quality of life better than when I was in The Netherlands?

At the end of the day I was single, I had no mortgage, no kids... Maybe it was just the best time in my life to do something more crazy and irresponsible. I love to backpack and I love to travel but I knew that doing that for a whole year would bore me, so my wish was to be in a place, have a routine and get a feeling of how it is to live in that place. I felt that that could be accomplished by being in a city for a month and carrying out regular activities while being there.

With that in mind, the idea to visit 12 months 12 cities started to take shape. I've already been to Cape Town, Berlin, San Francisco, Florence, Copenhagen, and Dubai. Still on my wish list are Sydney, Seoul, Tel Aviv, Teheran, New York, and London.

So far, San Francisco is my favorite: I love the atmosphere, the tech scene, the people and their lifestyle (interesting work, sports, healthy food and it's a bit of a party town). The natural surroundings are amazing, and each afternoon there is something fun or interesting to do.

By the time I took my sabbatical I was mentor at Startup boot camp. I kept my commitment and remotely mentored the teams as much as a I could, and traveled to Barcelona when necessary to support the teams. I enjoyed doing this very much so I started to offer myself as pro-bono mentor to mobile app startups in the city that I lived in. This ended up being fun, interesting, and it allowed me to get view each city from a different angle and meet different kinds of people. It was a great way to keep my knowledge up-to-date, as I would dive into problems that I truly enjoyed figuring out.

I would not call myself a digital nomad. I did make some money during my trip but almost accidental as it was never my intention to do so. My trip was more a gift to myself, as I had never had done a trip after my studies. Some people my age chose to do an MBA as a kind of break, but I had already done that, so my preferred choice was to just explore.

GIVING BACK/VOLUTEERING

Sooner or later, digital nomads realize how lucky they are to live the life they are living. Sure, they may have had to overcome some challenges to get to where they are, but there are billions of people in the world who are not able to move around freely, or who have to struggle to make ends meet.

By no means are we suggesting that digital nomads should feel guilty for their lifestyles. On the contrary, chasing happiness is a good thing, while spending money in a foreign country (when done in a respectful way and at local businesses) contributes to the local economy. Even without making a conscious effort, digital nomads are making the world a better place.

However, you may be one of those nomads who like to take their contribution a little further. They are not happy just spending their money, but want to do something meaningful while they are visiting.

There are many ways to do this. Usually an opportunity to help, however small, presents itself if you are open to it. For example when Esther was in Rio de Janeiro while writing this book, she met Fabio Rondinelle, an ex-drugsdealer who now organizes tours in the favelas and visits to projects offering street kids alternatives to the drugs trade. She was so touched by his motivation and passion, that she decided to help him with his (very primitive, self taught) website inktour.wordpress.com. Esther wrote some English copy for Fabio, asked his previous clients for recommendations and paid for a Portuguese WordPress expert from Fiverr.com to improve Fabios website skills. To Fabio, not only the new contacts, skills and content mattered, but "the fact that a foreigner cared at all, lifted my spirits and gave me new motivation".

Volunteering

Whether it's teaching tech skills, volunteering at an animal shelter, or doing refugee work, there are many 'voluntourism' opportunities, some of which can easily be combined with online work.

One way to find a volunteering job is through word of mouth and by knocking on doors. Someone you meet at your destination is bound to know someone who works for a shelter, temple, NGO, church, school or orphanage. Any help may be welcome, although there are organizations that require a minimum commitment, or even a financial contribution, from volunteers.

If you prefer to plan ahead, you can look for volunteering opportunities online and then decide whether to travel to a certain area or country. The following networks are suitable for finding a way to 'give back' to the world.

Workaway.info seems to have the largest list of host families, guesthouses and other organizations looking for volunteers and offering something in return. Anyone can look up the listings, but it requires a paid account to contact hosts. At the time of writing, the price is €23 for single travelers and €30 for couples, which provides you access for two years.

On **Help Exchange** (helpx.net), you can find farms, homestays, ranches, lodges, and even sailing boats, where volunteers are welcome to work in exchange for accommodation and in many cases also food. You may be required to work two to eight hours a day, depending on the offer. You can join for free, but it costs €20 for a two year pro membership.

WWOOF.net is an abbreviation for World Wide Opportunities on Organic Farms. WWOOF hosts exchange accommodation and food for your help. For a few hours of work you will get a place to stay and (organic!) food. A great opportunity to learn about a sustainable lifestyle, too.

Of course you need to check health risks of the places you are planning to visit, take your shots, protect yourself against mosquitos and use condoms. This information can be found online and in travel guides like the Lonely Planet. In this section we'd like to share some 'weird and geeky' digital nomad tips on how to stay fit and healthy.

If playing sports and maintaining a fitness routine can already seem challenging when you're living in one place, imagine the discipline that is required for working out on the road! Most health advice involves fixed routines. The lack of such routines is exactly what makes digital nomad life so interesting. But to fully enjoy our lifestyle, we need to stay fit.
While you can't, and shouldn't, guess the duration of someone's trip by their Body Mass Index, it is generally true that the nomadic lifestyle, with all its restaurant visits, increases our calorie intake.
Here are some ideas for –and examples of– ways you can avoid illnesses, keep your weight in check, stay fit, and remain flexible, during your adventures.

MEDITATION
It is important to take time for reflection. Find your own way to relax. Some prefer walks in nature, others practice yoga or some form of meditation. The app HeadSpace.com is a nice introduction to meditation. It is your very own personal trainer for the mind. Learn online, when you want, wherever you are, in just 10 - 20 minutes a day. This app offers a free ten-day program.

BE KIND TO YOUR BACK AND NECK
Much overlooked is the strain that our backs, necks and shoulders experience from bad posture. Hunching behind a laptop for hours on end tightens the muscles and pushes the vertebrae in unnatural positions. Getting up and moving regularly, stretching, and weight training can help compensate for this. Or, why not end your workday with a visit to the local yoga or Pilates studio? Take advantage of the cheap massages in many parts of the world and treat yourself to one weekly. Your back will thank you for it.

BODYWEIGHT EXERCISES

Of course you want to stay in shape on the road. But will it take al lot of time? Do you need to become a member of a gym? Do you have to hire a personal trainer? Or bring half a gym in your suitcase? With the 7-minute workout, the answer to all those questions is NO.

In 12 exercises, using only your body weight, a chair and a wall, this workout fulfills the latest mandates for high-intensity effort, which essentially combines a long run and a weight room workout into about seven minutes of steady discomfort — all of it based on science. Download from the App Store: bit.ly/7min-workout

1. Jumping jacks   2. Wall sit   3. Push-up   4. Abdominal crunch

5. Step-up onto chair   6. Squat   7. Triceps dip on chair   8. Plank

9. High knees running in place   10. Lunge   11. Push-up and rotation   12. Side plank

Freeletics.com is another popular app, which helps you exercise without weights, anywhere, anytime you like.

FLEXIBLE GYM PASSES

When you 'slow travel', getting a gym membership makes sense. But when you spend short periods of time at destinations, it's not worth it to become a member of a gym. If you miss the buzz, the social aspect, and/or the motivation a gym provides, there are solutions. More and more gyms are becoming part of (inter)national networks that allow you to access various locations with one pass.

One of these is ClassPass.com. A monthly membership of this network allows you to join the classes that work for you, whether that's Bikram yoga, or cycling and circuit training. Thousands of classes in 31 cities in the US, Canada and in London are available.

Holmes Places has gyms in 8 EU countries, and Israel. Many gym franchises, like FitnessFirst or McFit, offer memberships that are valid in all gyms in the country, or even internationally.

Germany has Somuchmore and Urbansportsclub, which offer various classes in places all over the country. In The Netherlands Onefit. nl offers access to over 50 gyms, yoga studios, dance schools and swimming pools in Amsterdam and The Hague. Get €10 discount using this code: bit.ly/onefitdiscount

SIGHT JOGGING

A fun and novel way to combine sightseeing and exercise, sight jogging takes you past the highlights of a city while you work out. You see more than on a conventional walking tour and meet like-minded people. Google 'sightjogging' and find guided tours in many destinations. Warning: Make sure your fitness level matches that of your guide, and vice versa. ☺

> *When I get to a new destination and I have internet access, I mark the place where I'm staying on Google Maps. If I don't have internet, I use the GPS app Citymaps2Go and mark my new home there, to prevent getting lost. Then I start my run through the city or nature. This run can often take more than 2-3 hours, but with a lot of stops for taking pictures, reading or speaking to people.*
>
> *I mostly try to let go and go with the flow. If there is any street or path that looks interesting to me, I just take it to see what I will find. That has already brought me to areas and places where I would probably never have come on a official sightseeing tour.*
>
> – **Suparni Neuwirth**, food blogger and yoga teacher (supi.life) –

DIETS

Since abs are made in the kitchen, some nomads take their diet very seriously. Inspired by Tim Ferriss's The 4-Hour Body and Loren Cordain's The Paleo Diet, many nomads shy away from processed foods, alcohol and carbs, instead loading up on greens, fish, and grass-fed meats. Some nomads will even go so far as to travel with a blender, so they can make their green smoothies anywhere they go.

BODY AND SLEEP HACKING

For a while, it was fashionable to experiment with nootropics, medicines that were meant for people who suffer from narcolepsy or dementia. A Modafinil pill was said to 'switch on' the brain for ten hours of focus, with no side effects, and without being addictive. Lately, internet entrepreneurs have jumped on the bulletproof coffee bandwagon. Dave Asprey, the blogger who came up with this controversial buttered coffee, claims that "you will experience the best mornings of your life, with boundless energy and focus."

And why not analyze your sleep cycles with an app like SleepCycle. com? It will activate the alarm clock when you're in the lightest sleep phase. In case you're worried, there is no need to strap anything to – or plug something into– your head; sleep trackers use the gyroscope in your smartphone to detect your movements in bed.

FIGHT JET LAG

You may need to make or take a call in the middle of the night. Your trip may involve a night flight, or you may have traveled so much that your body has no idea where in the world you are or what time it is. Some say you should adapt to the new time zone as soon as possible; others say that you have to listen you your body and take a nap whenever you feel like it. Find out what works best for you. Melatonin pills will help you sleep and adapt quicker to the new time zone. Worth a try: the acupressure routine that helps many to reduce the effects of jetlag. bit.ly/acupressure-jetlag

Bad news: the older you get, the harder it is to adjust to nights in planes, time and climate differences, and irregular sleep cycles.

MORNING RITUAL

Ever since Hal Elrod did his rounds of the popular business podcasts, his Miracle Morning has been selling like hot cakes. In this book, the motivational speaker proposes a morning ritual that will make you start your day like a superhuman: meditate, repeat affirmations, visualize, exercise, read and write.

KEEPING YOUR FOCUS AND INNER PEACE

★ Simplify your life. Discard unused stuff, and only spend time, money and attention, toward what, and who, is really important to you.

★ Avoid stress. Don't take life so seriously. Try to laugh about the things that happen and the mistakes you make. Whatever you're going through, how you react is a choice.

★ Create moments of mindfulness. Enjoy each moment, and the world around you.

★ Plan to let go. If you have your life in order, it is much easier to relax. So plan and work ahead.

★ Live more positive. Focus on the things that go well, with lower expectations, and more appreciation.

DIGITAL NOMAD HOTSPOTS –
WHERE TO LIVE, WORK & PLAY?

Since this subculture leans heavily on geo arbitrage (that is, taking advantage of currency and price differences between home country and destination), most digital nomads end up traveling to developing countries. Southeast Asia is a favorite for its low cost-of-living and high internet speeds. Destinations in Central and South America are becoming popular too.

Digital nomads who experience a certain level of success, or those who have savings to support their endeavors, tend to pick more developed countries: the USA, Australia, New Zealand, Singapore, Hong Kong, South Africa, the UK, Germany, etc.

Cost-of-living and internet speed are, of course, important parameters, but there are so many more factors that may be important to you when it comes to picking your next destination. NomadList.com helps to compare digital nomad hubs. Fed by crowd sourced data, this database allows you to filter cities and islands by climate, quality of nightlife, female friendliness and safety, just to name a few.
We recommend to always take your decisions based on a combination of sources. Many sites are still relatively new, and the quality and accuracy of data will improve as more user data is submitted.

Below are some of the 'hottest' digital nomad hubs. For more hotspots, we happily refer you to Webworktravel's Travel Guide for Digital Nomads: webworktravel.com/travel-guide

Chiang Mai
In what may be the 'digital nomad capital of the world', you will find farang (foreigners) tapping away on laptops in every cafe in town. The fast Wi-Fi speeds, the low costs-of-living, the high levels of safety, and enough entertainment options to last you months, make Chiang Mai an ideal base for beginning digital nomads. Join Chiang Mai Digital Nomads (facebook.com/groups/cmnomads) for news and tips on living in –and working from– this city in Northern Thailand.

Bangkok

Chaotic but fascinating, Bangkok gives you the full city lifestyle, with great food, swanky rooftop bars, a bustling startup scene, and lots of expats. You will probably end up spending a little more than in Chiang Mai, but your options in coworking spaces, luxury apartments and things to do are virtually limitless. Bangkok is a direct flight from most European capitals, and there are lots of transport options to other Thai towns and islands.

Bali

Popular with the yoga and surf crowds, Bali is a more low-key destination that has also been labeled 'Southeast Asia for grownups'. One of the best-known coworking spaces in the world happens to be in the town of Ubud. Hubud.org is a bamboo office with its own 'healthy cafe' and views of the rice paddies. On an almost daily basis, Hubud organizes events, ranging from Indonesian language classes to skill-sharing sessions. There are even workshops for budding digital nomads. You can stay in Hubud's 'The Villa', or easily find your own accommodation.

Tarifa

Tarifa is a small fishing town in Southern Spain, with a very beautiful old town center, surrounded by nature. It is close to Morocco, car rental is very cheap, and the internet is quite fast. April to June and September to November are the best months to be in Tarifa.

Largely thanks to the efforts of Johannes Völkner, who runs the Webworktravel.com blog and a Facebook group for digital nomads (bit.ly/facebook-webworktravel), the town of Tarifa has become somewhat of a hotspot for (mainly European) digital nomads. Strong and constant winds in Tarifa invite kite surfers to hit the endless beaches, while the local bars make perfect work places.

> *I stayed in an Airbnb apartment with a Russian kite surf teacher. I worked mostly from there, but through the Facebook group 'Tarifa Digital Nomads' (bit.ly/dn-tarifa) we were all connected, posting about where to meet for a working session, or just to have dinner or drinks.*
> – **Suparni Neuwirth**, food blogger and yoga teacher (supi.life) –

Tarifa. Photo: Stella Romana Airoldi

Canary Islands

The Canary Islands are part of Spain, but lie off the coast of Southern Morocco in the Atlantic Ocean. Blessed by a subtropical climate, and surprisingly low cost-of-living, they attract tourists year-round. In the European winter, they are your best bet for flip-flop weather.

On the island of Gran Canaria, Las Palmas is a big city with a splendid beach. This is where The Surf Office (thesurfoffice.com) branched out. Startups and location-independent entrepreneurs work from the city's many coworking spaces and cafes.

The island of Tenerife, famous for the world's second-biggest carnival celebration, has spectacular landscapes and centuries-old towns. Coworking in the Sun (coworkinginthesun.com) in Puerto de la Cruz also offers accommodations and Spanish lessons to digital nomads, while coworking spaces in and around the island's capital of Santa Cruz are great places to connect with local freelancers and startups.

Berlin

For sheer numbers of digital nomads, Berlin beats any other European city. Especially in the summer months, it draws nomads from all over the world, adding to an already lively community. With many coworking spaces and hip cafes to choose from, and reasonably low costs-of-living, Berlin is a good place to lay your laptop for a while. Start-ups in creative fields like design, fashion and art, add to the alternative vibe.

Bulgaria

Bulgaria is one of Europe's cheapest countries and also has low tax rates. It has bustling beach resorts and ski slopes, quaint villages and an interesting cuisine. Bulgaria ranks high in tables of internet connectivity speeds as well, making it an interesting (temporary) home base for location-independent workers.

Amsterdam

With the Netherlands' superfast internet, Amsterdam knows many trendy cafes with Wi-Fi, coworking spaces, and tech startup communities. Mix that with the historical city's history, culture, night scene, liberal mentality, canals, bicycles, and people, and you have a wonderful destination. Late spring, summer, and early fall are your best bets for good weather, which is a must if you want to ride your bicycle through the city or the rest of the country.

Mexico

"When traveling north through Central America, Mexico feels like coming home," André likes to say. "Buses have air-con and Wi-Fi, there are lots of shopping malls and ATMs around, and the food is delicious." These small luxuries don't come at a high price. Mexico is budget friendly and is easy to get to from the US. Down south, on the Yucatán peninsula, Playa del Carmen is becoming somewhat of a nomad favorite. Check out how this beach resort compares to Chiang Mai in this blog post (bit.ly/cm-vs-pdc). Other Mexican towns that are drawing the location-independent crowds are San Cristobal de las Casas and San Miguel de Allende.

Colombia

Medellín probably takes second or third place in the digital nomad hotspot rankings (being a close call with Bali). It's not difficult to see why: the country was voted 'happiest country in the world' in 2012 and 2015, the economy is booming, this university city is always up for a party, has a mild climate and enables an affordable lifestyle. Wi-Fi is ubiquitous and fast, and you'll find lots of coffee shops and juice bars to work from. The city draws a lot of male hopefuls because, reportedly, the women are gorgeous, too.

Vietnam

Vietnam is not only a wonderful country to visit, but is also a great source for cheap labor. We're not talking sweatshops, but rather refer to highly educated and talented programmers, developers and designers. If you are hiring help from Vietnam, you have another good reason to visit this country with its 2,000-mile-long coastline. Big and bustling Ho Chi Minh City, and charming coastal town Hoi An, are prime digital nomad destinations in Vietnam.

HOW TO MEET OTHER NOMADS

If you felt like an 'outsider' back home, you'll be disappointed that you'll often feel the same way while traveling. Sure, you'll meet lots of people, both locals and expats, and maybe even some travelers. Still, digital nomads are few and far between. The point is, every now and then you just want to hang out with like-minded people. Other digital nomads with the same needs, who face the same challenges, and enjoy the same activities. But how do you find these other nomads, and where?

First of all, let's not forget the power of friend referrals - Often when I'm traveling somewhere, I'll post it to Facebook and ask for recommendations and people will intro me to their friends. There's no stigma around meeting a stranger for a pint anymore.
– Josh –

When you are trying to figure out whether this lifestyle is for you, visiting a conference or going on a workation or a retreat is probably a good idea. You can experience the digital nomad lifestyle in a safe environment within a specific period of time. You'll meet other aspiring nomads and people already 'living the life', who can help you get a better idea of what it is like.

MEETUPS & GROUPS
In a big city, there's a meetup for everything. Many places frequented by location-independent entrepreneurs have their own meetups.

- ★ Meetup.com is a good starting place for finding formal and informal gatherings.
- ★ Overview of 49(!) digital nomad meetup groups: digital-nomads.meetup.com
- ★ Startup meetups: bit.ly/DN-startups
- ★ The Dynamite Circle (bit.ly/dynamite-circle) has various juntos worldwide. From time to time, tens to hundreds of DC members will move to a city to work and party there for a few months. Ho Chi Minh City, Chiang Mai, and Barcelona, have had this honor before.

- ★ CoWorking Spaces - Even if you're not a member of them, there will be event listings in their buildings.
- ★ Couchsurfing.com also organizes meetups and events. It's not our first choice, but many nomads say they've met some cool people through their meetups. Note that some businesses will list their events too (like paid pub crawls - not everybody's scene).
- ★ Many nomads use Tinder and other dating apps and sites, bars, etc. to meet both locals and other nomads.
- ★ There is a LinkedIn group (50 members): Digital Nomads and Location Independent people: bit.ly/DN-linkedin
- ★ Nomad List Slack Channel - There's a few travel slack channels, but this is the most active: hashtagnomads.com has groups for most popular cities around the world.

Being in an online community with other location-independent people is very informative. When I got to Ho Chi Minh City one month ago, the members who were already there were able to tell me which SIM card was the best choice, where to find the best work spots, where I should go to extend my visa, or where to buy stuff for my laptop. At other times, it had happened to me that I was the first to get to a destination, which gave me an uneasy feeling, as it took a lot of time and effort to get everything sorted.
– Jurgen Dhaese, copywriter (jurgendhaese.com) –

Facebook groups: Many travel, nomad, mobile entrepreneur, and digital nomad groups, are popping up on Facebook. We list the biggest and most popular ones below.

* WebWorkTravel - Digital Nomad Network (almost 8K members): bit.ly/fb-webworktravel
* Digital Nomads around the world (almost 6K members): bit.ly/fb-dn-atw
* DNX community (almost 500 members): bit.ly/fb-dnx-community
* NOMADS a live of cheap/free travel (110K members, not all digital) bit.ly/fb-nomads
* Remote entrepreneurs (300 members): bit.ly/fb-remote-entrepreneurs
* NomadList page (almost 8K likes): bit.ly/fb-nomadlist
* Local Digital Nomad facebook groups, like Chiang Mai Digital Nomads (8k members bit.ly/fb-cmnomads) or Gran Canaria Digital Nomads (800 members bit.ly/fb-gcnomads). Just search "CITY" digital nomad and you'll find one.
* Local language groups like 'Wereldburgers' in Dutch (350 members): bit.ly/fb-wereldburgers
* Expat groups: just search 'expat' and the name of the city you're in of Facebook and you'll find various groups.

ONLINE COURSES & FORUMS

What would be a better place to find fellow digital nomads than online? Some online forums require a paid membership, while others offer free access.

* Thefreedomplan.rocks is a paid course by 'suitcase entrepreneur' Natalie Sission. It consists of 12 modules and comes with access to a closed Facebook group.
* DigitalNomadAcademy.com, by digital nomad blogger Cody McKibben, includes a business 101, mentorship calls, and an active forum.
* LocationRebel.com, by digital nomad Sean Ogle, offers step-by-step blueprints for different location-independent, freelance jobs. The members support each other on the forums and Facebook group.
* The Dynamite Circle (tropicalmba.com/dc) is a private community of online entrepreneurs. Run by the guys behind digital nomad blog and podcast, Tropical MBA, it welcomes freelancers and entrepreneurs who are already successful and who want to take their business to the next level. Membership is on an invitation-only basis.
* #hastagnomads (hashtagnomads.com) is a digital nomad forum initiated by NomadList founder Pieter Levels. The one-time fee for joining this community is $65.

CONFERENCES

Whether you've been on the digital nomad trail for a while or you're looking for inspiration before you take the plunge, a conference is a great way to surround yourself with hundreds of other location-independent workers and entrepreneurs. They are often held in attractive locations, so why not take a tax-deductible trip?

Apart from the inspiration and the stellar networking opportunities that conferences offer, you can learn about the newest internet marketing techniques and programming languages in the presentations and workshops.

- WorldDominationSummit.com – Gathering of remarkable people in Portland (USA) each summer. Organised by Chris Guillebeau, the presentations and workshops during WDS help answer the question: How do we live a remarkable life in a conventional world?
- Pioneer Nation is another Chris Guillebeau event in Portland. "The world is changing as more people choose to work for themselves. We're inviting independent entrepreneurs, small business owners, and freelancers of all kinds to join us for a three-day strategy session." pioneernation.com
- DNX Global (dnxglobal.com) is a conference for and by digital nomads, with speakers, workshops and socializing opportunities. The first edition was held in Berlin in 2015 and the second edition in Bangkok (March 2016).
- The Dynamite Circle organizes an annual members-only gathering in Bangkok with inspiring presentations, mastermind groups, and breakout sessions. DCBKK is usually held in October, the beginning of the 'cool season' in South East Asia.

WORKATIONS & RETREATS

You don't have to become a nomad to enjoy a location-independent lifestyle. Some freelancers, entrepreneurs and investors choose to have a fixed base, but travel a few times per year, taking their laptop to beautiful places.

A number of o-called 'workations' have popped up that cater to this kind of worker. The concept is simple; location-independent workers can visit a new location and work from a shared space, while meeting other online entrepreneurs with a passion for travel.

Whether you want to see if the digital nomad lifestyle is for you or whether you simply need some sunshine in the darker winter months, a workation offers inspiration and is sure to expand your professional network.

While there are differences between the retreats in terms of accommodation and daily schedules, all aim to find the perfect balance between work and play, promising inspiration, productivity and fun. A typical workday during a retreat may consist of a healthy breakfast, a work session interspersed by dips in the pool, lunch, a siesta, some more work, sports before a BBQ dinner, and a showcasing of each other's work after dinner.

* HackerParadise.org packs ups and leaves to a new destination every other month or so. In 2015 alone, this project offered retreats in Bali, Barcelona, Berlin, Vietnam, Thailand, Tokyo and Taiwan.

* Refuga.com started as a Danish-language workation, but soon embraced international guests. These workations attract "entrepreneurs, athletes, artists, CEOs and other proactive people for adventures across the globe." The aim is to change mindset, ambitions, and perspective.

* Flaks.nl, originally a Dutch workation, is now spreading its wings and welcoming international guests. The main focus is on kite surfing, other (water)sports and yoga.

* Similarly, DNXCamp.com sticks close to the sea or ocean, with watersports as a recurring theme. Organized by Marcus and Feli of digital nomad conference, DNX Global, the focus is on lifestyle design, with life, work and play, taking place in luxury villas.

* Coworking-Camp.com holds one or two workations per year. The organizers like to pick large hotels for these events, with earlier editions on Egypt's Red Sea coast and on the Tunisian island of Djerba.

* ProjectGetaway.com runs month-long workations in Balinese villas, attracting entrepreneurs and freelancers from all continents. Their in-house app allows guests to order a fruit smoothie with a tap of their fingertip. Chefs and cleaners make sure no time is wasted on chores.

* Originally a German initiative, Sunny-Office.com has attracted guests from all over Europe and beyond. With five to seven international events a year, participants can choose one or two-week stays. The organizers have joined forces with Coboat.org for a unique Maldives workation in 2016.

COLIVING PROJECTS

Imagine you're a single traveler and you're thinking of visiting a new place. Wouldn't it be great if you could land at the destination and immediately be surrounded by like-minded nomads? By starting off in a coliving space, you feel at home from the beginning, while giving your business a boost, by brainstorming and networking with fellow online entrepreneurs.

Whereas a workation or business retreat is usually of a fixed duration on a pre-determined date, a coliving space allows you to move in and leave whenever you like. It may be an apartment within walking distance from a coworking space, or it may be a villa with more luxury and comfort than you can handle.

★ TheSurfOffice.com (coworking and coliving) started out in Gran Canaria (Canary Islands). Founder Peter Fabor wanted to escape Prague winters and be closer to the waves. His bed-desk-surfboard concept was so successful that it spurred the opening of a branch in Santa Cruz (California) and another one in Lisbon. "The most important thing we realized is that Surf Office is not that much about surfing anymore," says Peter. "It's about the community of people who kill the routine and enjoy their lifestyle."

★ NoHatDigital.com is a project in Valle del Bravo, on the shores of Lake Avándaro (Mexico). They invite online entrepreneurs to join their community, in a mansion with a private chef. Their mission is "to create opportunities for people to earn a full-time remote online income and live and work with a community of peers." There are lots of sports in the area, and owners Hayden and Han organize excursions on weekends.

★ Sun-Desk.com is a coworking and coliving space in the Moroccan surf town of Taghazout. The work area on the second floor has views of the Atlantic Ocean. "To keep focus levels high while working, we keep the coffee supply strong and constant, as well as providing lunch options, snacks and healthy refreshments," the website states.

✴ NomadHouse.io, on Bali, invites web developers, bloggers, drop shippers, anti-bosses, startup founders, renaissance revolutionaries, freedom philosophers, and financial hackers, to join its workation camp. This four-bedroom villa is situated on the hills outside Ubud and has previously hosted a Hacker Paradise retreat.

And once you have found your own paradise, why don't you get a long-term rental and open your own coliving space? On CoNomads.com, you can find people who are either interested in joining a coliving space or in starting their own.

CRUISES

Digital nomads take working from anywhere very seriously. They have been seen taking foldout chairs and tables into the mountains for some quiet work time. They drive around Europe in their campervans, using mobile Internet to stay connected. It seemed only a matter of time before they would hit the high seas, since even in the middle of the ocean, internet is available to those who are willing to pay for it.

Not that you need to be connected 100% of the time. For many, brainstorming is more effective when they put the old-fashioned pen and paper together. Design work can be done offline; you can record beautiful videos with the ocean as a backdrop; you can write content and plot out your professional course for the months ahead. This is exactly what Niall Doherty found out when he crossed the Pacific on his round-the-world-without-flying challenge. At the end of his maritime adventure, he had written a book.

In some cases, boarding a yacht or ship can be cheaper than staying home, as in the example of the repositioning cruise. Mostly, however, traveling by boat requires a healthy budget or reliable income stream.

Repositioning cruise

In October and November of 2015, two cruise ships with over 150 digital nomads crossed the Atlantic Ocean. Each fall, Spanish cruise company Pullmantur (bit.ly/repositioning-cruise) repositions its ships from Spain (Las Palmas) to Brazil (Salvador), and in the opposite direction for the winter season. For what is a 7-night ocean crossing with no land in sight, Pullmantur charges an incredibly low €154 per person. With internet connections costing €0,20 per minute, this trip was mostly a digital detox for those on board. This doesn't mean that no work was done. Passengers spontaneously organized mastermind groups, held presentations, elaborated business plans, and more. Esther wrote a blog about the experience: bit.ly/cruise-your-business and created an online training about productivity with two other location independent entrepreneurs on the cruise: GetShit-DoneCourse.com

Johannes Völkner of Webworktravel did a great job of mobilizing European nomads and created nomadcruise.com to organize more of these popular cruises.

Live-aboard catamaran

Late 2015, a catamaran, with up to 20 digital nomads, set sail in Southeast Asia, making its way to Europe and eventually the Americas. Solar and wind-powered, equipped with satellite internet, the Coboat visits islands and coastal towns, allowing passengers to hop on and hop off. Coboat.org is an initiative by four nomads who met in a coworking space in Koh Lanta. You can book anything between a one-week and a one-year stay.

German-born Marcus Meurer (1977) and Feli Hargarten (1981) run a German travel blog and organize digital nomad conferences and digital nomad workations around the world.

Felicia (Feliciahargarten.com) and I started by freelancing for clients. We built websites for companies and consulted them in online marketing, PR and communication. Then we started the professional travel blog Travelicia.de, which is now one of the biggest travel blogs in Germany. Growing a website to the point that you can live from it takes time. Now we could easily live just from the travel blog, but in the beginning our freelancing work enabled us to travel full-time.

In the past few months we started to grow our team and hired our first virtual assistant (VA). Before that, we already had a designer and translator working for us, supporting us in our different projects. Quickly we realized how important the decision was to hire a VA. We gained confidence and brought more freelancers on board and set up workflows for different tasks. Right now we have 15 location independent freelancers working for us regularly. Our team is fully remote and we all work in different timezones. Working with a team gave us back the headspace we needed to take our business to the next level.

When I started my first own projects it felt like breaking the chains. There was so much energy, creativity and power in me that I couldn't help starting more and more projects. At a certain point you have to calm down and focus on what is really important and could change the world. Discovering that entrepreneurial fire is nearly better than sex... ☺

One of my biggest productivity hacks is setting up routines and structure. The first hour of my day is scripted: I wake up with sunrise, I am an early bird. I make my bed which gives me the first win of the day. Sports activate and energize me: I do the 7 minute workout with functional training. After sports I meditate for 20 minutes with the Headspace app. While drinking a green smoothie for breakfast I write in my 5-Minute Journal (Fiveminutejournal.com).

Then I start the day with my Most Important Task (MIT). The trick is not going into your emails or social media accounts before that. When you finish your MIT you already won the whole day!

We began the DNX movement to connect and support digital nomads all over the world.

One of the key success factors for us online entrepreneurs is to surround ourselves with like-minded people. That keeps us motivated and helps us to take off into that lifestyle. Also digital nomads who already travel the world need like-minded entrepreneurs to ping business ideas and take their projects to the next level.

We started the DNX digital nomad conference (dnxglobal.com) in Berlin to gather like-minded people from all over the world. It was a huge success with 450 people from 34 different countries. The next DNX Conference is in March 2016, in Bangkok, Thailand.

In 2015 we also started coliving and coworking camps with 15 digital nomads for 10 days in the most beautiful places all over the world: DNXcamp.com. Right now I am in Brazil where the next DNX CAMP starts tomorrow. We already run CAMPS in Tarifa and Lisbon and will do more in Thailand, Bali, Santa Cruz and other stunning places. During the DNX CAMPS people get even more connected and we do lots of DNX talks, workshops and masterminds.

The digital nomad movement is shaping the future of work. The movement of location independent entrepreneurs, freelancers and employees is speeding up all over the world. This means there will be more and more people going on the road and work from anywhere. One-hundred percent remote companies like Buffer, Automattic and Toptal understand that remote work is a big opportunity and game changer. Companies that adapt quickly to the new way of working have a big asset in the battle for talents on the job market. Digital nomads will be world changers in all different digital topics. We are well-connected, share our knowledge and have a 360-degree perspective from traveling the world.

 www.marcusmeurer.com

AND NOW IT'S UP TO YOU!

WHERE WILL YOU GO?

WHAT WILL YOU DO?

THE WORLD IS OUR PLAYGROUND.

HAVE FUN!

"The memories you want for tomorrow must be made today."

ESTHER JACOBS

Esther (The Netherlands, 1970) is an international speaker and author. She gave more than 1000 keynotes, inspiring entrepreneurs and decision makers of organizations like Capgemini, Hewlett Packard, KLM, Phillips and universities on 5 continents. She published and contributed to 16 books.

As a pioneer and entrepreneur Esther became an expert in getting results with limited resources, especially in challenging circumstances. The "No Excuses Lady" proves that you can turn even the bleakest situation into an opportunity:

★ Raised $25 million for charities without a budget, network or experience. Got knighted by the Dutch Queen.
★ Survived a reality TV show on a deserted island.
★ Turned her relationship with a playboy into a bestselling book: 'Have you found your Mr Wrong yet?'
★ Got 'fired' from her country for traveling too much; became a digital nomad, living and working in 100+ countries. The very government that expelled her, is now consulting her on how to solve this issue for future mobile generations.

Esther occasionally takes a group of entrepreneurs on mastermind sessions in exotic locations. Check her workshops, books, RESULTant sessions and inspiring newsletter on www.estherjacobs.info

ANDRÉ GUSSEKLOO

André (1980) studied Tourism Management, but ended up freelancing as a self-taught copywriter. In 2012 he decided to celebrate his location-independence with a temporary move to Thailand. In 2014, his girlfriend Marta chose to do a yoga teacher training in Costa Rica, prompting a five-month trip through Central America.

Now living on Lanzarote with his baby boy, André teaches SEO copywriting (www.beachwriter.net) to those who wish to be location-independent themselves. André is currently working on several books in the travel, business and self-help niches. He is also available for presentations and workshops. You can follow –and contact– him through his personal blog: www.andregussekloo.com.

Made in the USA
San Bernardino, CA
22 September 2017